The

*Gift*

of

Grandparenting

The
*Gift*
of
Grandparenting

Thea Jarvis

 SORIN BOOKS    Notre Dame, Indiana

www.sorinbooks.com

International Standard Book Number: 1-893732-63-0

Cover design by Eyecreate/Bill Ferguson

Text design by Brian C. Conley

Printed and bound in the United States of America.

*Library of Congress Cataloging-in-Publication Data*
Jarvis, Thea.
    The gift of grandparenting / Thea Jarvis.
        p. cm.
        ISBN 1-893732-63-0 (pbk.)
    1. Grandparenting. 2. Grandparent and child. 3.
Grandparents.  I. Title.
HQ759.9.J37 2003
306.874'5--dc21

                                                            2003007152

*FOR MY FAVORITE*
*DANCING PARTNER*

# Contents

# CHAPTER ONE

# A Time to Play

I live on a small barrier island off the Georgia coast. My husband and I moved here from Atlanta just before he retired some years ago. One of the things we like best about our new home is that it's a stable, viable community. Lots of people vacation here because it's a fine place to visit, but there's a civic and social life that exists outside the comings and goings of the tourist crowd. There's plenty to do, much to see, ample opportunity to contribute to and take part in the energy of island life.

Despite the island's obvious charms, I had anguished over our move chiefly because it was a five-hour drive from our children and grandchildren. On some primal level, it felt like I was abandoning them. At a time when they were feathering their nests, making them safe and warm for a future they hoped would be bright and fruitful, Mimi and Papa were pulling up stakes. Bailing out. Running away. Or so my darkest thoughts seemed to tell me.

Happily, this hasn't turned out to be the case. We make the drive to Atlanta at least every other month for some event in the busy life of our growing family. If it's not a birthday celebration, it's time to erect a backyard shed or check out a new playground set. We're there when the babies arrive or when older siblings need attention. Sometimes, we're on the road just because we need a hug. Our grandchildren haven't forgotten who we are, our children haven't disowned us, and we haven't yet languished in isolated decrepitude. At the same time, our offspring have found that relaxing with their children here on the island is a good way to unwind and spend time with their larger family. Our chosen place of residence has become a getaway destination, a place of rest.

"When you move to a cool place," a wise grandparent once assured me, "your kids and grandkids can't help but visit." In the words of the popular saying, *If you build it, they will come.*

This island is awash in grandparents. It's also awash in grandchildren: big ones on scooters, little ones on trikes, babies in strollers or snuggled securely in their grandparents' arms. Grampy can be sighted walking the shoreline in ragged shorts, faded tee shirt and beat up sneakers, holding the hand of a beachcomber barely a third of his height. Despite their difference in size, the munchkin is in the lead, dragging Grampy closer and closer to the water, where both sets of sneakers are ultimately met and conquered by the incoming tide. No matter. The child, doggedly intent on his journey of exploration, barely notices. Grampy, transformed by the presence of his miniature companion, dwells in a state of quiet euphoria. His wrinkles have turned up into a grin that takes ten years off his face. His eyes twinkle like the sun on blue water. His chest expands with the salty air and the pride he's feeling in the little person leading him around like a trained seal.

A few steps back, Nana follows with her own retinue. She doesn't hold their hands, but the gaggle of grandchildren leaping around her looks like a swarm of seagulls awaiting a taste of fresh flounder. Nana's grin is modest. She knows she's got it all and doesn't want to gloat. Clad in a bright fuchsia jogging suit that's too tight around the hips and a pair of zippy running shoes she bought on sale at Payless, Nana deftly reaches for the ball her grandchildren have been passing back and forth to each other. "Got it!" she hollers, giggling like a teenager. "Bet you didn't think I could!"

Whether they know it or not, Nana and Grampy, like most grandparents on this island, have discovered one of the biggest payoffs grandparenting has to offer. At a time in their lives when they thought they'd be sitting in a rocker watching the world pass them by, they are goofing around like a couple of unruly schoolkids. Unconscious of the arthritic shoulder Grampy pulled playing golf last week or the headache Nana awoke with early this morning, these grandparents are down in the trenches, knee-deep in the mud, unwilling to miss this chance to dance in the sand with their new best friends: their grandkids.

It's a delightful surprise, this playtime granted in our later years. It's a built-in excuse to do the things we might have missed along the way. Or perhaps a chance to revisit activities we once enjoyed but have been too self-conscious or too weary to resurrect. When you're a grandparent, you don't have to hold back or hold off; your grandchildren move you forward, laughing and teasing and encouraging until caution is thrown to the wind and you can jump in, feet first, with a smile on your face.

My father's mother managed to do this in the literal sense. Nanny, a native New Yorker, loved to shop but had an aversion to escalators. Each Easter, Nanny sprung for new outfits for her grandchildren—not a small expenditure in our family of four girls and two boys. Her generosity was always appreciated, and we girls invariably crossed our fingers that, come Easter morning, a spring snowstorm wouldn't take the starch out of our fussy frocks and bonnets.

But getting from the store to the frock and bonnet stage wasn't easy because of Nanny's escalator phobia. To avoid her mechanical nemesis, this usually brave and staunchly independent woman would determinedly search out an elevator to ride or staircase to climb while we tagged along sulkily behind her. In

the fifties, these musty, old-fashioned con-
veyances were generally hidden well back in
the store, near the credit and gift wrap depart-
ments, or behind an exit door that was far too
heavy for small hands to open. We bore with
Nanny for years, but some of us grew bolder as
we moved into adolescence. During one pre-
Easter buying spree, our patience grew thin.
We whined and cajoled and kidded until our
poor grandmother was at her wit's end. "You
can do it, Nanny. You can ride that escalator,"
we bullied. "If we can do it, you can do it too!"

Today, the memory of pushing my silver-
haired grandmother into the jaws of the menac-
ing metal monster on Gimbel's second floor
doesn't make me proud. Gripping the handrail
like a life preserver on a sinking ship, Nanny
managed to hold fast as we surrounded her
with our bodies and our cheers. "Just a little
way to go, Nanny," we chorused, trying not to
notice her quivering knees and frozen, terrified
face. "We're almost to the bottom!"

And when we got there? Well, let's just say
that Nanny appeared to have crossed her own
Rubicon. "I think we should do it again," she
gamely volunteered, her knees still knocking,

her feet still unsteady in her black lace-up oxfords. "I don't want to lose the momentum." By the end of the day, Nanny was a pro, riding those escalators like Coney Island roller coasters. We half-expected the store manager to break out the cotton candy each time Nanny landed safely at the foot of the moving stair. Shopping for Easter outfits became a secondary pleasure in a day that was filled with playful moments and Nanny's gleeful satisfaction that she, too, could master the ups and downs of the modern department store.

Nanny's husband, my father's father, knew no such fear of modern conveniences. In fact, the only thing Grandpa was really afraid of was mustard. He'd been overcome by mustard gas in France during the First World War and the mere smell of the spicy condiment sent him running for cover. Grandpa was always picking up odds and ends he'd find at local thrift shops: old radios and kitchen tools, salvageable toys and sporting goods. In the finished basement of Nanny and Grandpa's modest home in the Manhattan suburb of Richmond Hill, my grandfather had installed a jukebox whose origin still remains a mystery to me and the rest of the family. It was a wondrous thing, this jukebox. As a child, I loved descending the narrow basement stairs to the cave-like room where music held sway. For me, the happy sounds pouring from the jukebox were overshadowed only by the sweet melodies that issued from Grandpa's mouth as he accompanied the machine with his own renditions of popular pieces.

We grandchildren, of course, were Grandpa's most devoted audience, a natural excuse for him to break into song. "Daddy's Little Girl" was my particular favorite. When Grandpa sang, "You're the end of the rainbow, the pot of gold. You're Daddy's little girl, to have and to hold," my eyes would fill and I could barely keep the tears from rushing down my face.

To sing to me as he did, to warble like a karaoke king and allow his lyrics to take root in my little girl heart, Grandpa had to let go of any self-consciousness that might have held him in check. He had to plant himself squarely in the moment and accept the freedom it offered. He had to reach up and switch off any negative messages that might have rattled around in his head: *This is too silly for an old guy like me. I sound like a parrot with a head cold. Do these kids think I'm nuts?* He had to follow his instinct and let his heart lead him on.

My grandparents, and most grandparents I know, discovered early on that it takes a certain humility, a measure of vulnerability, to play with your grandchildren. Grandparents must be willing to let down and get down, to put so-called serious issues aside, to take off their top hats and put on their clown costumes. Some are better at it than others.

My friend Marilyn welcomes the break her grandchildren give her when they come to town. While everyone around her is fussing over meals and worrying about schedules, Marilyn lets such trivialities slide so she can be present and available to the grandkids she loves so much. Because a grandchild's connection with a grandparent exists in a finite bubble of time and space, nothing is more important to her than enjoying the hours spent with them. "I only have so much energy to spare," she explains. "What I have, I want to give to them."

I confess that this is something I've had to work at. Order and routine are important in my life; they keep me feeling safe and secure. A serene and peaceful home, I have found, contributes to a level of peace and serenity within myself. But when grandchildren are introduced into the picture, feathers start flying and order quickly loses ground to chaos. My quiet routine gives way to high comedy and light opera, a sometimes confusing, always surprising turnabout. Little by little, however, I'm learning to accept and appreciate this intergenerational interplay. Moreover, I'm starting to embrace the pleasantly chaotic turn my life can take whenever my grandkids explode on the scene. Like Marilyn, I've discovered that not much else is as important as they are.

If grandchildren are expected, I clear my calendar and disappear from the social scene. "You won't see me for a week unless we run across each other in the park," I tell my friends. I stock the pantry with Cheerios and animal crackers and make sure the laundry isn't backed up to the neighbor's front door. I dig out a collection of old toys and update our small library of children's books in the extra bedroom. I shake out the sand toys and foam surfboards hidden somewhere in the garage, and uncover a cache of metal cars and trucks my parents found at a yard sale one spring. Preparation is all-important if I hope to carve out some playtime with my grandchildren.

A child-sized oak table and chair set we used for our own children still does duty for the little ones. It's a sturdy, useful spot for an afternoon snack or a turn at the coloring book and crayons we have on hand. I put up breakables that can't be replaced and clear away newspapers and magazines to make way for the inevitable paraphernalia grandchildren seem to manufacture. The result? I'm ready for action, loaded for bear. I'm available and approachable—an aspirant to that heavenly state of grandparental bliss that routinely kicks in when a grandchild puts her hand in mine and murmurs, "Play with me, Mimi."

A favorite place to take my grandchildren is the park. We have several within walking distance of our house, each with a generous assortment of climbing and swinging equipment. One park overlooking the ocean has a miniature golf course that's a handy diversion on hot summer nights. Though jungle-gyms aren't my preferred choice of exercise contraptions, I love to swing. Having a grandchild around is a perfect excuse to backtrack to girl-hood and the swing sets of my youth.

"Into the clouds, into the trees," I croon, pumping my blue-veined legs with abandon, often with a child on my lap. If I'm the designated pusher, I'll stand in front and grab my grandchild's toes to make him giggle. It makes me giggle too. The unfettered chuckle of a grandchild is laughter like no other.

Have you ever danced with a grandchild? Like swinging, it's a form of play and produces laughter of a rare and matchless variety. I may have gotten my sense of rhythm from my father, who won more than his share of dance contests in his youth, but I learned the intricacies of dancing with small children from my mother, who was her grandchildren's favorite partner. The ritual now known in our family as The Dee-Dee Dance is relatively simple.

I grab a small child from his parent's clutches and grasp him tightly in my arms. Keeping eye contact, I place my right arm gently around his waist and raise my left hand so my palm is facing out, towards the child. With a big dumb grin on my face, I invite the child to dance.

"Want to dee-dee?" is a passable request. I pay no attention to the titters of adult onlookers or the initial mask of bewilderment on my grandchild's face. The wisdom of my actions will soon be revealed to the doubters and I will, literally, have the last laugh.

Repeating my invitation to dee-dee several times, I lift the child's right hand and entwine it in mine. Eye contact is critical to evoking the laughter that will eventually erupt from the child in my arms. I begin a slow polka step (that's a one-two-three beat in case you've forgotten) and loudly sing the following to the tune of "The Beer Barrel Polka."

> *Deedle-ee-dee, deedle-ee-dee,*
> *Deedle-ee-dee-dee-de-dee-dee,*
> *Dee-dee, de-dee, de-dee-dee,*
> *Deedle-ee-dee, deedle-ee-dee.*

Singing the verse over and over, I dance in exaggerated steps around the house with my grandchild. When I can no longer stand up, I close with the following:

> *Dee-dee, dee-dee, de-dee-dee*
> *Deedle-ee-dee-dee-dee-dee. Hey!*

By the end of the dance, my grandchild is laughing or, at the very least, grinning in wonderment at my stamina. To continue the laughter, I start over from the top. A colorful finish is a graceful fall onto a couch, with my grandchild hugged tightly to my belly. If I pretend to snore, the flow of laughter will be non-stop. Fortunately, this dance is easily adapted to older grandchildren, who frequently find that dancing with a grandparent is a great excuse for a giggle. Older kids have a fine sense of the ridiculous and there's nothing quite so funny as their grandparents dancing a polka in the living room.

My brother Jim has more energy than I do. He not only enjoys an occasional turn around the dance floor, but can often be found cavorting on the snowy slopes of Vermont while his weak-hearted sister keeps company with the fireplace logs. Not long ago, Jim, already an accomplished skier, became certified to teach the gentle art of snowboarding to novices. His grandchildren are reaping the rewards of their grandfather's adventurous spirit.

Jim's oldest grandchild, Erik, has recently been introduced to the wonders of the downhill.

He's not yet ready for a snowboard, Jim tells me, but he's a rock and roller on kiddie skis. While Erik's dad gives him a gentle nudge from atop a small hill, Jim awaits his grandson at the bottom. Legs akimbo, Jim calls out the challenge: "Come down and ski between my feet, Erik." His grandchild thinks this a great joke, as does his Pops, who manages to jump out of harm's way just as Erik finishes his run.

"The most fun is seeing him have fun. It's pure delight," Jim reports. What's more, time spent with his grandson is an outlet for my brother's boundless energy and exuberance. "Erik is somebody to go out and play with on the mountain," he says. "That's really what we're doing—playing."

Happily, Jim's caught on to the Zen of grandparenting, the joy of release, the gift of the moment. When you're with a grandchild, says my brother, "you're not worried about anything else that's been troubling you. You can just focus on him," letting the world and its burdens take care of themselves.

A short block down the street from us, there's a vintage cottage that looks as if it had been torn from the pages of a fairy tale. Its white clapboard siding is accented by narrow green shutters and an aging shingled roof. An arched trellis of bougainvillea frames an uneven stone path leading to a brick stoop and old-fashioned front door. It's not a large house, just a single story, but the backyard is ample and has a shady oak canopy and a small fishpond. There's a large live oak in the front yard, too, casting its protective arms above a house known to locals and visitors alike for its pride of place in our village preservation district. A small oval sign near the front stoop officially designates the cottage as *Grandma's House*.

The house is stocked with enough antiques and memorabilia to make a collector like me squirm with envy. Old letters and linens, vintage kitchen decor and utensils, well cared for furnishings from the thirties and forties invite guests to step back in time, remember the past, and feel welcome.

The sign by the front door reminds the owners, two sisters who inherited the house and lovingly keep its memories intact, of their childhood and the idyllic summers spent in their grandmother's home. The island was their playground, they tell me, and they remember Grandma as a lighthearted playmate who loved to share their days. Her spirit lives on in the house, which now accommodates family visitors and a second generation of lucky grandchildren eager to explore the island's nooks and crannies.

Grandma's House is a good reminder for me as well. Each day as I pass it on my walk to the ocean nearby, I am encouraged to make my own family memories, to designate my home as a place where grandchildren are welcome. Where they can come to play. And where I can play too.

---

*Grandparents at play with their grandchildren can release their self-consciousness and live fully, completely in the moment. Playing with a grandchild absolves us from the past and frees us from the future. We become one with the present, at peace with ourselves.*

## CHAPTER TWO

# A Time to Teach

*NO ONE HAS THE RIGHT TO SIT DOWN AND FEEL HOPELESS. THERE'S TOO MUCH WORK TO DO.*

*Dorothy Day*

I learned to drink tea at my grandma's house. Great gobs of tea, softened with milk and served with sweet rolls or shortbread biscuits that were a perfect fit for my small, freckled fingers. Drinking tea was a grownup thing to do, something that made me part of a larger world where adults talked about important things like the McCarthy hearings or the neighbors' new Buick. I felt welcome and safe at my grandmother's table.

Tea time was a family ritual. A fruit-bordered cotton cloth was laid on the dining room table and the kettle put on to boil atop the kitchen stove. China and flatware were always used; paper plates were unknown and would have been unwanted. Tea was taken with lunch and just before bedtime. At breakfast, too, if we wanted it. We drank from delicate cups with flowered saucers and were hardly aware of the gentle nourishment we were given, so naturally did it flow from my grandmother's capable hands.

Grandma wasn't a high-flying sophisticate. The mother of twelve, widowed during the dark days of the Depression, she had taken in laundry and ironed other people's clothing to put food on her family's table. She soldiered through challenges that would have made a drill sergeant weep and had a dry sense of humor that surfaced in the direst of circumstances. Strong and wise, with a mind quick to grasp complexity and nuance, Grandma was a living testament to her strong Irish genes and a faith that never faltered.

But Grandma knew that presentation was important. Setting a table with taste and attention to detail spoke of love and care and the belief that others were worth the effort. Little things mattered, Grandma's tea time told me. And little people mattered too. The days spent in my grandmother's home were filled with a deep sense of security and the knowledge that I was loved just because I was me. I knew I was a special part of Grandma's life because everything she did for me told me so.

I still drink tea today. Great gobs of it. I use lemon and forego the milk and sugar, but tea remains number one on my hit parade of drinkable delights. If you come to visit, I'll offer Earl Grey or Irish Breakfast, maybe even some of the triple echinacea green tea I found at the health food store. In summer, I'll serve tea over ice, with orange and lime and garden mint if it's available. You see, tea, for me, says: *Welcome. Make yourself at home. Pull up a chair and chat for awhile. I like you. You're special. You're worth the time for a cup of tea.*

Not surprisingly, I've started serving tea to my grandchildren. Not the heavy-duty, super-caffeinated stuff of course, just a little taste of their grandmother's tea now and then. Milk and sugar make it more of a treat and some cookies on the side are always appreciated. Indulging in such adult fare denotes privilege and status. And giving a bit of tea to my grandchildren reminds me that I can pass on the blessed gift my grandmother gave to me: the sense that my grandchildren are valued and loved for themselves alone.

Teaching a grandchild her importance, her special place in my life, is perhaps the greatest gift I can offer. Whether drinking a cup of tea together or kicking around a soccer ball in the backyard, the message I want to convey is that I think she's a superhero, a marvel, a doer of great deeds and thinker of great thoughts, a grandchild of weight and substance. In this way, I become a benevolent contributor to my grandchild's growth and development, encouraging her to accept and love herself simply because she is who she is.

My neighbor Bill sends this message to his grandchildren over a pool table. In fact, Bill and his wife Mickey designed their retirement home with a pool table at its center so Bill could shoot pool with his children and grandchildren on a regular basis. This arrangement, you understand, implies a large and loving grandmotherly heart as well as a grandfather's noble desire to bond and connect with his grandchildren. It is at the pool table, cue stick in hand, that Bill lets his grandchildren know he's crazy about them. There, they not only realize that they're on the short list of pool players Bill invites into his inner sanctum, but they also learn, with the benefit of their grandfather's able experience, the finer points of a corner shot. All this activity, of course, is happily fueled by hefty injections of soda and chips from Grandma Mickey's ample pantry.

Over time, the pool table has become a gathering place for Bill and Mickey's grandchildren. The boys are more apt to participate, but the girls are on deck, too. The kids along with their friends, dates, and random companions have all discovered the welcoming warmth that surrounds them when they walk through Bill and Mickey's back door. At the same time, my neighbors have earned the satisfaction that comes from giving their grandchildren irreplaceable gifts of time and interest.

My own children's Gram, my husband's mother and my mother-in-law, sent subtle messages of unconditional love to her grandchildren over countless games of cards. For me, taking time for a card game when laundry piles threaten and dinnertime looms is the hapless pursuit of lollygaggers and lunatics. But Gram deemed such prodigal behavior entirely appropriate, even meritorious. Playing cards with her grandchildren, teaching them the rules of old maid, was for her the most sensible and relaxing of pastimes. Her small body straight and poised as a princess, she sat through unending hands of gin rummy and war as if she were conducting affairs of state. Her dark eyes focused on her grandchildren's upturned faces; she guided her little orchestra with an invisible baton. Time with her grandchildren, her patient demeanor implied, was music to her soul, as important as any household task, any book she might be reading, any movie she could be watching on television.

One of my children's happiest memories is their Gram's perennial willingness to spend time doing what *they* wanted to do, when *they* wanted to do it. Another round of cards? Not too much to ask when a grandchild was making the request. Gram was intuitively responsive, enfolding her grandchildren in an extravagance of attention, an abundance of pride.

"You won!" she'd announce while I busied myself in the kitchen, awe-struck by my mother-in-law's uncanny ability to fulfill pint-sized dreams and tiny wishes. Today, I remember Gram's lessons of patience and grace as I find myself playing endless rounds of board games or cards with my own grandchildren. It must surely be her spirit that props me up when my jaw goes slack and my eyes begin to glaze over.

Now, playing pool or rummy might not be in your repertoire of grandparental abilities. You might even disdain tea. But we all know it's not the activity that's important, it's the exchange. We're not teaching our grandchildren *to do* so much as we're teaching them *to be*. We're teaching them how much they count in this world and how valuable they are to themselves and to others. In this way, grandparents offer a radical, often counter-cultural message that it's the person, not the performance, that counts.

My friend Bebe is an organist at our church. She has oodles of grandchildren because she had oodles of children. How she keeps up with them all is beyond me. Bebe's youngest granddaughter, Megan, is the one I know best. On those Sundays when she visits her grandmother,

Meg can be found sitting next to Bebe on the organist's bench. When services begin promptly at ten-thirty, Megan stands quietly by her grandma's side and turns the pages of music Bebe uses to accompany the choir. It is the gentlest of interchanges: a shy, somewhat solemn young girl making herself available to a dedicated, silver-haired musician. Only whispers are allowed—it's church time, after all. But the link between the two is apparent to those who watch them together.

*Megan*, says Bebe wordlessly as her fingers dance over the keys and her feet plow the pedals, *I'm so glad you're here today helping me with my music. You're doing such a good job and I'm so proud of you. I love you very much.*

*Grandma*, Meg replies with her eyes, trying hard not to notice the crowd of people massed in the pews, perhaps looking at her, *I like being here, helping with your music. It makes me feel important. I'm happy when I'm with you because I know how much you love me.*

Teaching grandchildren their value and worth is a privilege conferred upon those who've been around long enough to understand

and appreciate the job. We grandparents aren't necessarily the smartest or wisest of beings, but we're usually more certain of our priorities. More often than not, we're blessed with the time and willingness to put those priorities into action.

When my father was asked by his grandson Michael to visit Mike's school for a day, he knew this invitation took precedence over any other engagements that might be pending. At the time, Dad was living on Long Island and Mike and his family were a few hours north in Connecticut. Not a problem, Dad had decided. He was retired and available. New York's notorious commuter traffic notwithstanding, Dad thought the trip would be a piece of cake. Moreover, he knew he'd get to talk to Michael's class about one of his favorite topics: blimps. Dad had flown these unique airships during World War II and had gazillions of old Navy stories to share. What better way to spend an afternoon? He could pour forth lots of interesting information few people were qualified to impart. At the same time, he could let his grandson know his grandfather wanted to be a significant part of his life.

Dad's classroom debut was a hit. Mike's classmates loved him. The teacher loved him. Mike was happy because his grandpa was someone he could be proud of, someone who cherished him and cared enough to show up just because Mike had asked. My father's willingness to brave the roads and stand in front of an audience of high-spirited fifth graders sent an unspoken message to his grandchild: *You're some special guy, Mike. The traffic was awful and these noisy kids are making me nervous, but you're worth it. I love you and I'm really glad to be here with you and your friends.*

My mother has been no less effective as a teacher and a grandma. Along with my dad, Mom has now reached the revered level of great-grandparenthood, a term that belies the energy and enthusiasm my octogenarian parents manage to generate wherever they go. From her early days as a grandmother, Mom made it clear that her grandchildren were the chosen people. She fussed over them like a brooding hen, making sure they ate right, dressed warmly, and blew their noses. They, in turn, loved their grandma. She could make them laugh, bake them cookies, and teach them stuff nobody else appeared to know.

Often, Mom would take her grandchildren to church. Sometimes, it wasn't even on a Sunday. Frequently, she brought along more than one child at a time. In the quiet interior of the aging building, Mom would invite her grandchildren to pray with her and always let them know exactly to whom they were praying. Our church had little votive candles lined up like sentries in metal racks at either side of the sanctuary. It was a dream come true for her grandchildren to accompany their grandma to church, where together they would light a match, set fire to some candles and not get arrested.

"Shall we go down to church and light a candle today?" Mom would suggest to her visiting grandchildren. Immediately, the lucky kids' eyes would begin to sparkle, anticipating the darkened church and the mesmerizing dance of flame in its crimson glass container. The experience combined delicious elements of scary movies and birthday parties. Their reply was predictable: "Yes, Grandma, let's go to church. Let's go now!"

My mother is a sainted woman, but she is adept at bribery—especially when it involves her grandchildren. Once inside the church, Mom knew she had a captive audience. The candle-lighting ceremony was carried out with due reverence and delight. Finger-scorching was held to a minimum. Afterwards, candles lit, Mom and the children wandered about the church like tourists in a museum, Grandma explaining points of interest to her wide-eyed grandchildren while injecting bits of simple theology along the way. Mom is a natural teacher and the kids warmed to her subject without realizing they were being exposed to such heady material. It was a time my mother set aside to share something deeply close to her heart with the young people she loved most in the world.

I confess to no great talents I can share with my grandchildren, no important instruction I can pass along. I did, however, have some modest success teaching my oldest grandchild how to somersault. Ray was visiting with his family at our house and quickly made his way to our bedroom, newly carpeted in a soft, off-white shag that was as inviting to a preschooler's heightened senses as a sheepdog's furry coat. Off went my grandson's shoes, down went his hands, in went his little-boy toes, deeper and deeper into the snowy carpet.

Before I knew it, young Ray was hot-dogging around my room, cavorting on the carpet as if it were a freshly mown lawn.

"Can you do a flip?" I inquired, intent on corralling this ball of energy and saving my just-painted walls. "Yes, Mimi," he replied and bent double, like an inverted vee, in front of me. "Very good," said I, encircling his waist with my hands. "Now, over you go!" His delight as he tumbled into a somersault was infectious. We laughed together at his success. "Let's do it again, Mimi," he begged.

And so we did, over and over. The new carpet survived our gymnastics and Ray became more and more confident of his somersaulting abilities. His feat was as gratifying to me as if I'd been the one doing the work. Best of all, Ray realized his grandmother thought him worthy of a turn on the virgin white shag and the time it took to learn to somersault.

On a larger scale, I have seen the difference such affirmation can make in the life of a child and in the world children inhabit. A recent trip to Cumberland National Seashore, the largest wilderness island in the U. S. and Georgia's southernmost coastal treasure, allowed my husband and me to glimpse the power of a grandparent's trust and vision. We had saved our pennies and stayed at Greyfield, a gracious turn-of-the-century mansion that opened to the public in 1962 when Lucy R. Ferguson, a granddaughter of Thomas and Lucy Carnegie, transformed her ancestral home into an inn.

While other voices had urged development of the island on a par with nearby resorts, Miss Lucy held the line on her heritage. She retained the homestead, honoring the dreams of her sizable brood of children and grandchildren, who had encouraged her to keep the venerable home and its two-hundred-acre site on Cumberland's south end.

"They think when I pop off, my eighteen grandchildren will get [into] a devil of a fuss and then it will be easy to acquire," Miss Lucy observed in a 1977 *National Geographic* interview when debate over Cumberland's future still waxed hot and heavy. Though developers coveted Greyfield's gracious bounty, Miss Lucy's example and the lessons she had taught her grandchildren meant the legacy was safe in their hands.

Today, Greyfield is operated by Lucy Ferguson's progeny. Her grandchildren, now with children of their own, can be found working the Greyfield ferry, creating art from island fossils, mixing easily with Greyfield guests. Wild horses roam the expansive grounds, mossy oaks form a canopy of shade for weary travelers, the river and ocean are near at hand. Inside, the house is welcoming, engaging visitors in a kindly embrace. Meals are served family style, picnics are encouraged. There's no pretense here, just the glow of quiet dignity, the warmth of open-armed hospitality.

On the west wall of the inn's handsome library, where vacationers gather for after-dinner coffee and pre-dinner delights, Miss Lucy is immortalized in an oil portrait that depicts her in classic pirate garb. A colorful bandanna on her head, a dagger on her hip, the lady of the house appears a formidable adversary to those who would threaten her family's heritage and Cumberland's extraordinary natural beauty. Viewing the portrait, it's easy to understand why her grandchildren, who see the island through Miss Lucy's eyes, do their part to maintain their grandmother's gift and share it with others who are humbled and hypnotized by Cumberland's rustic charm.

Miss Lucy's grand inheritance isn't mine to give; her resources are beyond my imagining. But her message to me, one grandparent to another, rings true: *Teach what you know. Give what you can. Let your spirit and your passion rise up and spill over, lighting a fire in the hearts of those you love.*

Sometime soon, I'll climb back on the ferry and walk the sandy trails of Cumberland with my grandchildren. I'll tell them about Miss Lucy and her family, show them the feral horses, maybe spot an armadillo or two on our hike to the beach. For now, though, back at home, I'm content to enjoy the teachable moments that serendipitously occur when my grandchildren are by my side.

Watching the birds at our backyard feeder, we'll listen for the song of God's creation. Walking the shore, we'll delight in the colors of the morning sky and the shapes of shifting clouds. Reading a book, we'll discover a new word and learn some funny riddles. Our hearts will open to each other and we'll dance together like old friends. Once again I'll be overwhelmed by the gifts my grandchildren bring me, once more be grateful for the times we share. And once more, I'll do my best to teach them, as my grandmother taught me, that they are loved without condition—just because they're my grandkids.

---

*Grandparents are full of small lessons grandchildren are eager to learn. In word and in action, we teach with the wisdom life's experiences have conferred. Most of all, we teach our grandchildren how important they are.*

## CHAPTER THREE

# A Time to Grow

*OUR PRIMARY PUR-
POSE IN OUR GOLDEN
YEARS IS NOT JUST TO
STAY ALIVE AS LONG
AS WE CAN, BUT TO
SAVOR EVERY OPPOR-
TUNITY FOR PLEAS-
URE, EXCITEMENT,
ADVENTURE, AND FUL-
FILLMENT.*

*Jimmy Carter*

While vacationing some years ago, I met a man who epitomized the kind of grandparent I hoped to be one day. He was the presiding docent on a coastal tour of Native American Indian ruins and I was fascinated by his grasp of complex archeological information. In a leisurely conversation after the tour, I learned our guide was an inveterate seeker, always on the lookout for new subjects and places to explore. It was important to him that his grandchildren experience the same wonder he felt for the world.

"On their tenth birthday, my wife and I let them choose a special place they'd like to visit," he told me. "Then, as our gift, we do our best to take them there." Naturally, if a child requested a flight on the Concorde with birthday cake to follow at a Parisian cafe, even these generous folks might have discouraged the fantasy. But if the dream were reasonable, affordable, and obtainable, their grandchild's wishes would be honored and celebrated. It was a creative way for these thoughtful grandparents to spend quality time with their grandchildren while fine-tuning their personal learning curve.

"Right now, I'm trying to get a couple of tickets to a Braves game," our guide had confided as we walked and chatted. "My grandson turns ten next month and he's dying to go." The frown on his face indicated that he wasn't having much luck. The Atlanta team was red hot and every fan within four hundred miles was beating his feet to the stadium. Fortunately, that year my husband had secured season tickets. At the time, we had no grandchildren of our own to indulge and occupy, but we often went to the ballpark with our kids, who enjoyed the games as much as we did. I asked when my new friend needed the tickets and said I'd check our stash when we returned home. He beamed in gratitude, a grandfather with hope renewed.

In the end, we sent him tickets for a game that matched his family's schedule. It was a pleasure to receive his gracious thank you, full of assurances that it would be one of the best birthdays his grandson ever had. Noshing on peanuts and Cracker Jack while players dance across a green diamond is a classic memory for a little boy. For this eager grandfather and his wife, it was one more chance to take a swing at lifelong learning.

Grandkids, I've observed, are a good reason to get out of bed in the morning. They're pint-sized coaches who cheer us as we ascend the slippery slope of our later years. Perfect excuses for a day at the beach or a walk in the rain, they're also convenient companions for a trip to the zoo or a history museum. Grandchildren are the leaven in our loaf, lifting us up, expanding our horizons, boosting our spirits with a word or a smile. Bribes for longevity, prods to action, grandchildren are the very ones to poke and pinch us when we're too comfortable on our couches, too set in our ways. *There's more to come, more to learn*, they impatiently insist.

Our good friend Jim is a single grandpa. As a retiree and a widower whose wife Anne was one of my closest friends, Jim is in charge of his life; his plans are of his own making. Jim's interests include visiting old pals like my husband and me, and making weekly runs to the city food bank so needy people can have something for supper. He's focused on family and is particularly involved in his grandchildren's lives. His grandson Christopher, now in his early teens, is a special buddy.

"Whenever he asks me to do something, I try to be available," Jim tells me. Because Chris' father was absent during his early years, Jim always made an extra effort to be around. Christopher now has a caring step-dad as well as a younger sister and brother who join him and his mom around the family table. But his grandfather is still number one on his hit parade. "He feels close to me," Jim is happy to report.

When Chris was eleven, it was his Pop who accompanied him to Space Camp in Huntsville, Alabama, where Chris' scout troop had gathered for a long weekend. Jim was the only grandparent on site, and, for the former Boy Scout, the weekend was an eye-opener.

"We didn't have the exposure they have now," Jim said of his own scouting experiences. "There were no out-of-state trips, nothing exciting. We just sat around a makeshift campfire roasting marshmallows and singing songs." At space camp, he told me, hands-on learning is standard fare for kids and grownups alike: intricate machines simulate space flight; deceptively entertaining games teach the rhythms of the solar system and the possibilities of planetary life. The first airships to enter outer space are housed in Huntsville, he'd discovered, along with historic photographs of maiden voyages and pioneer pilots.

"Every time I go anywhere with Chris, I'm learning something," said Jim, a willing student when his grandson is the teacher. Jim's learning isn't limited to scout camps and museums, but is an ongoing process that continues whenever he and his grandson are together. "Regardless of the age difference, I often feel we're on the same level," my friend confides. "We carry on like a couple of old pals." Chats with his grandson include talk of girls, God, sports, and Jim's late wife. "Sometimes in the middle of our conversation," Jim quips, "I have to ask myself, *Who's the grandparent?*"

Chris is a regular at his grandfather's house, where he often stays the night and spends Saturday mowing the lawn, grabbing lunch at a neighborhood restaurant, and taking in an afternoon movie with his Pop. It's a different experience for Jim, who had no close relationship with his grandparents while growing up. Even with his own children, he reflected, "Working two or three jobs meant I didn't always have time for them." With Chris, he senses, things can be different. "I always want him to know that I love him and that I'll be there for him," Jim said. "I want that door to be open."

The traditional bonds between grandparents and grandchildren have been enhanced by technology and by the lengthening of our days. Because we're living longer, we have more to learn and more time in which to learn it. With advances in communication, personal growth comes more quickly and easily. How many phone and cable companies advertise special rates so grandparents won't miss the details of a grandchild's spelling bee? How many curious grandparents are navigating the internet and mastering the art of e-mail so they can communicate with grandchildren across the country and around the world? How many brave-hearted seniors willingly negotiate the dizzying maze of major airports, lugging heavy suitcases and bulky carry-ons just to feel a grandchild's small sweaty palms around their necks? Grandparents today are doing more, seeing more, learning more. *Jump in or get left behind*, the world seems to be telling us.

Elderhostel, the international not-for-profit group that features educational and travel experiences for the fifty-five and over set, now advertises programs with an intergenerational twist: *When did you and a favorite youngster last visit a wildlife sanctuary to see bears and mountain lions close up?* an Elderhostel ad asks potential participants. *Have you ever studied the heritage of*

*Irish mythology while immersed in the charm and history of County Cork?* These are opportunities for grandparents and grandchildren to get to know each other, suggests Elderhostel, and such programs dovetail nicely with the organization's optimistic belief that "sharing new ideas, challenges, and experiences is rewarding in every season of life."

It's true. Life and growth don't stop at thirty-nine. If grandparents are natural learners, maybe it's because our edges have been softened, our defenses have been worn down, our arms are now open to receive whatever gifts life wants to give us. My own experience bears this out.

One weekend, when our first grandchild was only a toddler and his parents had escaped on a mini-vacation, my husband and I found ourselves in charge of their house, their dogs, and their precious baby. Over the course of four days, we tackled some lessons not studied in our previous lifetime.

The first morning of our stay we rushed out the door to ferry our sleepy grandson to preschool. Unfortunately, I had forgotten how long it takes to coax a little boy into shoes and socks. I'd also blocked out the agonizing ritual of getting through breakfast. *Would you like some milk, sweetie, or just plain Cheerios? No, we don't have any Sugarmallow Crispy Treats. Just the Cheerios. Ah, well, I don't think there's time for pancakes. Maybe tomorrow. Maybe for lunch. Maybe you'd like to eat in the car?*

In our haste to be on time, the house keys were left behind on the kitchen counter. I was, in fact, the last one out the door and neglected to bring the keys with me. My husband was the innocent party, dutifully studying the configuration of the car seat so our grandson could ride safely across town. "We'll deal with the keys when we get back," my chagrined but patient spouse decreed. Upon our return, we checked each door and window, only to find that our son's home was well secured, safe from potential burglars like ourselves. His two dogs, hunkered down in the fenced backyard, lazily watching our movements, barked at us now and again in solidarity.

As we scanned the upper story of the house, wondering how we'd tell our grandson he'd be camping under the stars and admit to his parents that we were unfit to serve, a possibility surfaced. That morning, after dressing our grandson in his new jeans, I'd left the window ajar to air out his room. The crack was barely noticeable, but was enough to allow entry to a couple of desperate characters like ourselves. A suitable ladder was discovered in the garage, and I held onto its cold aluminum legs while my husband bravely climbed to the roof. Grateful that age hadn't hobbled us, relieved that the neighbors weren't whistling and catcalling from their doorways, I began to laugh uncontrollably. Even my husband cracked a smile. I scrambled for a camera before the moment eluded us. After all, how often do you break into your grown child's home without getting caught?

That night, we served a celebration dinner of macaroni and cheese. It was the only food our grandson would eat and he devoured it like a cross-country truck driver. I shoveled noodles into his little pink mouth while he inspected the peas I'd added for protein. Those tiny green balls fascinated him. They were colorful, squeezable, the perfect size for his small, groping fingers. They were also the perfect fit for his little snub nose. Looking us straight in the eye, he popped a pea into his nostril with deliberation and care. It sat there like a misplaced puzzle piece.

"What do we do now?" my husband asked no one in particular. I was too panicked to answer. My only thought was: *Don't inhale.* We had made it through the big lockout. We'd even discovered that breaking and entering in the middle of the morning doesn't necessarily land you in jail. Wasn't that enough for one day?

Our grandson continued to stare at us as if we might have some constructive ideas about what to do next. By now he'd obviously decided that a pea in his nose wasn't the best idea he'd had all day and was hoping to have it removed. He didn't cry or whine, just blinked his eyes and stared at his befuddled caretakers. As the pea moved slowly up his nose, his stubby forefinger began exploring the site. Clearly, it was time to act. *Emergency room, paramedics, Q-tips?* Options are limited when an errant vegetable makes its way into a grandchild's head.

"Blow it out, honey," we counseled in well modulated voices. "Don't worry. It's going to be all right." Who were we kidding? While my husband went for the phone and I began to work on my grandson's nose, the little guy began a series of quick snorty exhales. The sound was barely audible, but resembled a puppy sneezing. *Fuff-fuff-fuff.* We watched in wonder as the pea suddenly shot from his face like a stone from a slingshot. Our grandson was still looking at us like we had some answers. Then he grinned slyly and our shoulders sagged in relief. Another notch on our belts.

The older I get, the less I know. Whether it's a pea up a kid's nose or a new way to catch fire-flies, I don't pretend to be an expert. As a grandparent, I'm always on the threshold of new growth. I don't want to be caught nap-ping.

An old Bill Cosby album, one my family found hilarious no matter how many times we heard it, featured a monologue on the startling change that had come over the comedian's par-ents once grandchildren entered their lives. The stern disciplinarians and finger-pointing overseers Cosby knew as a child were barely recognizable to him. They'd gone soft, he main-tained, clucking over his children's missteps like indulgent visitors from outer space, crowing at their smallest accomplishments like a couple of Hollywood promoters. Cosby couldn't believe the changes grandparenthood had wrought in the gray-headed strangers he once knew as mother and father.

"These people are not my parents," he sputtered helplessly. "They're just two old people trying to get into heaven." Mr. Cosby had it right. It's the job of grandchildren to shape their grandparents into more attractive versions of themselves. As a grandmother, I'm more patient and hopeful, more generous and kind. My sense of humor is looser, my sense of acceptance deeper. I have more respect for myself and understand better what faithfulness entails. These virtues blooming like flowers in a hidden garden aren't necessarily a reflection of my own wonderfulness. They're just proof that personal growth usually occurs when the title of *grandparent* is conferred. Some of the more obvious changes include:

*Patience:* Those fingerprints on my window, the handprints on my wall are badges of honor, a fellow grandparent reminds me. Remnants of recent visits from my busy grandchildren, they're signals that I'm growing and changing. A quick swab with cloth and cleaner easily removes the dirt. If things are really bad, there's always a can of paint in the garage. What isn't so easily removed is a harsh word or impatient gesture, signs that diligent house-keeping is far too high on my priority list. Time and patience are singular gifts I give to my grandchildren. How remarkable that those are the gifts they give to me as well.

*Self-esteem:* My granddaughters love to hide in the folds of my robe and inspect my pink-painted toes with curious fingers. They giggle when I scoop them into my arms and whirl them around like miniature airplanes. My grandson plays cards with me; his brother plays catch. They think I'm funny when I tell a new joke or talk like Donald Duck. If you notice a spring in my step, a smile playing around my mouth, maybe it's because my grandchildren have shown me that I am lovable.

*Acceptance:* Grandchildren are like pizzas. There's one in every size and flavor; one in every thickness I could possibly imagine. Variations on the basic model are never-ending; each serving is always a surprise. But the secret sauce that links my grandchildren together binds them to me as well. They're family. I accept their unique personalities, the quirks and habits that distinguish one from another, knowing that their delicious differences nourish and fill up my spirit.

*Humility:* Though I sometimes aspire to be the token grandparent on a *Leave It to Beaver* rerun, such stardom is destined to elude me. My feet are planted firmly on the earth; wings haven't yet begun to sprout from my shoulder blades. I get mad, sad, tired, hungry, irritable, and ugly—sometimes in the presence of my grandchildren. "We're not in heaven yet," a friend advises. I'm a humbler person, honestly acknowledging my flaws and weaknesses, because grandchildren help ground me in reality.

*Hope:* When I read the daily paper and turn on the six o'clock news, I'm tempted to bolt the doors and crawl under the bed with my teddy bear. The pictures aren't pretty and there are too many of them. Gazing into the eyes of my grandchildren is a different story. There, I'm treated to a vision of hope and promise. Their bright little bodies squirm with energy, their faces light up with expectation and enthusiasm.

How can I think the world is doomed when these wonders of creation are living in it?

*Courage:* I'm terrified of lightning and wary of big, burly strangers. I avoid heights and any sport that involves jumping, diving, or skiing from altitudes over three feet. I'm not exactly a pushover, but I'm not the bravest person I've ever met. My grandchildren, however, give me courage. With their hands in mine, I am Wonder Woman. Super Girl. I laugh at trouble, scoff at danger. Big dogs and people with green spiky hair don't bother me. At least, my grandchildren don't seem to think they do. When I pretend long and hard enough, I find that courage makes a home in my heart.

*Humor:* "I spy a color and it is red," my grandson said one day as he played the age-old game with his grandfather. As I entered the room, he gave my husband a broad hint: "She's wearing the color and she's very, very old." Looking down at my blazing attire, I realized he meant me, his apparently aging grandmother. As my daughter-in-law said when the septic tank overflowed: "If we don't laugh, we'll cry." Some things are so funny they end in tears. Some things are so awful they end in laughter.

Grandchildren have an uncanny ability to distract and entertain. Their antics may range from heartwarming to hilarious, from off-color to embarrassing. But whenever my grandchildren are around, they tickle my funny bone and sharpen my sense of the absurd.

*Awareness:* I love working crossword puzzles because they keep me totally focused and grounded in the present. The world virtually disappears as I ponder wordplay and definitions, quotations and double meanings. Grandchildren have the same effect on me. Totally absorbed in the now, they emit an infectious sense of immediacy to everyone around them; they're magnets for positive thought. How can I worry about tomorrow's dentist appointment when it's time for a walk in the park? Was last night's call from a pushy telemarketer really so annoying? Do I absolutely have to clean the bathrooms today? Time moves on, whether I want it to or not. *If you miss this moment*, my grandchildren remind me, *it will be gone forever.*

Some years ago, when I was overwhelmed by the logistics of moving to a new home in another part of the state, my sister offered some helpful advice. "Change is good," she told me. "It may be difficult, but it's good." My sister's own geographical upheavals had been for the better, she had found, though they often stretched and broadened her in places that were sometimes stiff and sore. "Change shakes us up, gets us out of our comfort zone," experience had taught her. "It breaks down old habits and pushes us forward, upward. It helps us grow."

Growth and change are operative at every stage of human life. Stagnation is not part of the plan. As grandparents, we're in process just as we were when we were teenagers or thirty-somethings. Happily, grandchildren facilitate and encourage the growth we're meant to have. They're pieces of our puzzle, colorful threads in the tapestry of our life. Without them, we surely might grow. But with them, our growth is guaranteed.

---

*Grandchildren are nature's way of telling us we're not yet ready for the bone yard. Growing and learning with and through our grandchildren, we realize our potential. Sometimes, we even fulfill our dreams.*

## CHAPTER FOUR

# A Time to Trust

*HAVE COURAGE FOR
THE GREAT SOR-
ROWS OF LIFE
AND PATIENCE FOR
THE SMALL ONES;
AND WHEN YOU
HAVE LABORIOUSLY
ACCOMPLISHED YOUR
DAILY TASK,
GO TO SLEEP IN
PEACE. GOD IS
AWAKE.*

*Victor Hugo*

Our first granddaughter arrived six-and-a-half weeks early. At the time of her birth, my husband was on a road trip to Denver with our youngest daughter, who had decided to give high altitude living a year's try. With all of her worldly possessions on board, my daughter and her dad were packed tighter than canned tuna into her little maroon sedan. Luckily, a cell phone was jammed in there too.

"Are you sitting down?" I asked when they phoned me from Pike's Peak. I was assured that they were, indeed, sitting down and had been doing so for no less than three days.

"Well, the baby's coming," I announced breathlessly. "Your sister's in the hospital and they can't stop her labor." Subtlety flew out the window as my brain downloaded both excitement and alarm. That cell phone, after all, could go dead any minute. "How soon can you two turn around and get back here?"

Throughout the day, our family burned up the phone lines. My daughter, who with the expected baby was now high-risk, called with regular updates from the labor room. My sons and daughters-in-law, attentive and concerned, relayed information to each other throughout the day. One of my sons, a physician, monitored his sister's progress through hospital staff, reassuring us that she and the baby were

getting the best of care. Our Colorado roadrun-
ners checked in every few hours for the latest
news bulletins.

I went to sleep that night feeling humble
and small. I knew there was nothing I could do
to help my daughter and grandchild. They were
surrounded by competent doctors and nurses,
supported by a loving husband and father,
buoyed by their own strength and courage. As
much as I wanted to be a key player in this
unfolding family drama, I realized my role was
a minor one. I was the understudy who had
dutifully memorized her lines, but had no
chance to deliver them. Even had I been with
my loved ones in the hospital, I understood that
their circumstances were beyond my control.
Ironically, my acute sense that the situation was
far too big for me to handle kept me grounded
in reality. I had no choice but to trust.

At times of significant stress I often find
myself praying in my sleep. I must have been
doing just that when the bedside phone awak-
ened me around four in the morning. The call
wasn't unexpected. It was my weary but jubi-
lant daughter announcing that Iris Michaela
had been born just minutes earlier, weighing in

at a surprisingly strong five pounds, four ounces. Relief and gratitude washed over me like a waterfall. I went back to sleep with a smile on my face.

Over the next year, however, I would have more opportunities to trust. I quickly learned that worrying about my grandchildren came as naturally as worrying about my children. Anxiety was a constant companion in those first few months of Iris' life. Trust became the reliable antidote, a self-medication that enabled me to move through each day believing that my granddaughter and her parents were guarded and protected by a power greater than they.

Like most premature babies, Iris was tested and retested, poked and prodded, hooked and unhooked to machines and probes. In my arms she was a tiny bird, a feather-child, a downy sparrow to be held and petted. Looking at her today—healthy, plucky, independent—it's difficult to remember how close we came to losing her. Yet on a warm summer night when Iris was just a month old, my daughter discovered her in the crib, struggling to breathe, her face and extremities frighteningly blue.

"I didn't usually turn on the light for her night feedings," my daughter later told me. But on that particular night, some instinct or intuition prompted her to press the switch, illuminating her baby's distress and imminent loss of consciousness. Our daughter and her husband followed the directions of a 911 operator, holding Iris' little neck at an angle to facilitate breathing. Paramedics arrived in time to stabilize the baby and transport her to the hospital for a weeklong stay. After extensive testing and observation, Iris was found to have a severe gastroesophageal reflux that had obstructed her respiratory tract and impeded her breathing. Diagnostics also disclosed the presence of a life-threatening, group B strep infection that had gone undetected because of Iris' prematurity. Two tiny holes were later found in her tiny heart.

At home, Iris was cared for with constant vigilance, lots of costly medication and an apnea monitor she was to wear twenty-four hours a day for nine months. We all spent the next few weeks getting used to the unfamiliar bells and whistles that now accompanied her high-tech life. Despite being mechanically inept and generally fearful of all things electrical, I learned to secure the Velcro straps around her little chest and correctly align the monitor's wiring. I also learned to interpret the digital signals and noisy emissions of the quirky machine that held my granddaughter's life in its hands. I learned to bless the man who designed the machine, himself the grieving father of a child lost to sudden infant death. And I learned to trust that the author of life was in charge of Iris' breathing.

The months that followed included more emergencies and hospital visits than I care to recount, interminable sleepless nights, and zombie days. Our eyes might have been full of sand, but our ears were attuned to the steady beep of the apnea monitor, which indicated that Iris was still with us. Gradually, she grew stronger. Her apnea abated as her reflux responded to medication. Her digestive difficulties improved as her insides matured. Her disposition lightened as her discomfort diminished. Clearly, Iris was blooming and flourishing. The first year of her life wasn't one I would have chosen for her, but in sharing my granddaughter's struggle, contributing what I could and leaving the rest to God, my own spirit was refreshed and renewed.

The decision to trust is not unlike swimming in the ocean in early summer. Who wants to go in? The water's too cold, the waves too high. Goose bumps cover my body and my bathing suit's shrunk at least two sizes since last year. Jellyfish are everywhere; crabs scurry underfoot. As I wade into thigh-high water, my teeth begin to chatter and I'm certain the brine is no place for a sissy like me. Turning around, I see the beach beckoning, a dry, sandy shelter, safe harbor for my knocking knees. But just as I'm tempted to head back to shore, to throw up my hands in total surrender, a grinning grandchild appears beside me. Laughing and splashing, she dares me to take the plunge. *C'mon, Grandma. It's not so bad. You'll feel better when you're all wet.*

All of a sudden, the water's a little warmer, the waves not quite so rough. I sink slowly into the salty bath, submerging my waist, my chest, my shoulders. With a giggle, I duck my head underwater and glimpse my grandchild's small round belly, which I quickly grab and tickle. Jellyfish scatter, crabs disappear. I release my fear to the wind and ride the waves like a happy dolphin, buoyed by a gentle current that supports and directs me. All at once I'm a kid again, a time-traveler, trusting and free.

The perspective of age and the wisdom of experience means that grandparents more easily sidestep their fears and hold fast to trust when trouble threatens. At their best, grandparents can be models of courage, beacons of hope in the face of daunting challenges and unexpected crises. Working through such events enriches us as well as the families we're part of. In the midst of them, we are validated and affirmed; the purpose and meaning of our later years becomes clearer. As we embrace and accept it, a larger plan unfolds.

Maria Carmela, our family's unofficial Italian grandma, embodies such courage. Born in Sicily over eighty years ago, Carmela came to the United States in her early teens and worked for much of her life in New York's historic garment district. A talented seamstress, she was a major asset in the designer showroom where she eventually found a niche and in the bridal salon at Macy's, where she held a second job to make ends meet.

Carmela's life wasn't an easy one, but trust poured out of her like water from an open spigot. A single mother with a limited mastery of English and little time for leisure, she was nevertheless able to send her only son to the best of private schools and universities. His academic gifts and Carmela's motherly counsel ultimately brought him to the U.S. Military Academy at West Point, where he remained to teach after graduation. Over the years, when difficulties arose, Carmela trusted that she and her son would be led and directed.

Carmela's ability to trust continues to astound me. Her faith is a solid yet accessible rock that she climbs each day and sits on like a queen, secure in the knowledge of its restful, restorative power. Carmela works as hard as she can and lets God do for her what she can't do for herself.

When her son married, Carmela looked forward to the blessings of grandchildren. She was, after all, a natural. My own children adored her, delighting in her warm, accepting personality, easy sense of humor, Old World cooking, and marvelous murder of the English language. For a long time, however, Carmela's grandchildren did not appear.

It was an absence she bore with dignity and a hope I couldn't fathom. Time certainly wasn't on her side; she wasn't getting any younger. My grandchildren had begun to arrive and I felt almost guilty knowing that I, the daughter Carmela never had, might outpace her. But my dear friend, then in her late seventies, continued to talk as if her expected grandchild were right around the corner. And just as she had predicted, just when I had given up the hope she'd never relinquished, Carmela *did* become a grandmother. After what seemed like an impossible waiting period, her son and daughter-in-law adopted a curly-headed, strawberry-haired baby whose coloring was an undeniable match for her grandmother's own fair hair and skin.

"She is perfect," Carmela proudly announced to anyone within shouting distance, "and so *intelligente*." How could I, a fellow grandparent, dispute her claim? When I met little Paulette, I had to agree. She was a charmer, a diminutive doll who, like the rest of us, was crazy about Carmela.

Today, Paulette lights up Carmela's world like a busy firefly. "She's in charge," her indulgent grandmother reports. When friends come to visit and Paulette is around, lunch is not a problem. "Let's go out to eat," she deftly suggests. When I call and Paulette is spending the day at Grandma's, it is she who picks up the phone and primly announces, "My grandma is taking care of me today." Whenever Mommy and Daddy come to speed Paulette home, she is reluctant to go. "Come see me soon, Grandma," she admonishes between hugs and kisses. "I will miss you."

Carmela is radiant, ever grateful, a joyful grandparent who knows her longstanding trust has paid off in ways even she couldn't have imagined. To Carmela, trust is a gift that never stops giving, a tool that never outgrows its usefulness. When shared with others, it puts muscle on the family tree, deepening bonds and softening trials. It's true that trust must be actively sought, mindfully chosen, Carmela will tell you, but in the end it's the easy way out. We grandparents may have our physical limits—our aches and pains, our wobbles. Yet, to the degree that we can trust, our emotional and spiritual energies know no bounds.

My old friends Joe and Joan have a large Polish-American family of four children and nine grandchildren. Their clan is now expanding exponentially as their beloved grandchildren grow up and begin families of their own. When Joe and Joan's granddaughter Amy was in her early twenties, her job landed her at the 1996 Olympics, where she was assigned to work long hours and late nights. On the face of it, Amy's employment was exciting and hip. Who wouldn't want to be at the center of Olympic action, meeting athletes and celebrities, basking in the glow of the global village? It was a young professional's dream. Unfortunately, it was also a nightmare for Amy's parents and grandparents, who were genuinely concerned for her safety. Often, Amy didn't finish work until the early morning hours, then faced travel to her suburban Atlanta home on a near-empty subway train. It was the scariest of situations, but my friends' hands were tied. There was nothing they could do to change Amy's circumstances. They could choose to worry or choose to trust.

Seasoned grandparents that they were, Joe and Joan knew the drill. They opted for non-resistance and turned Amy's nightly excursions over to the care of their God. Praying earnestly for Amy's safety, confident that their granddaughter would thus be protected from urban predators and marauding Olympic crowds, Joe and Joan were nevertheless surprised when a knight in shining armor showed up during Amy's first week of work. Brad, a fellow employee, was delighted to assume the role of Amy's escort and guardian, offering comfort and companionship on the long journey home. Over time, their relationship blossomed. Brad and Amy became a steady couple.

Later, when a detached retina landed Amy in the hospital, Brad was by her side, ever the protector. Doctors advised surgery to restore Amy's vision, but warned that risks were involved: paralysis, loss of sight, hearing damage. The crisis became a turning point in the couple's relationship. In tears one day, because of the inevitable operation and the dire consequences she might have to face, Amy was consoled by Brad's love and loyalty.

"He told me that he loved my soul and would always take care of me," Amy recalled. Brad was, unquestionably, the fulfillment of her grandparents' dreams. And as it turned out, he also had a surprising link to her grandparents' past.

"Brad's father owned a camera store in the little town where my grandfather did business," said Amy. "Grandpa remembers calling at the store and seeing Brad behind the counter, still in diapers. It's quite a coincidence that the little boy my grandfather met years ago ended up being the answer to my grandparents' prayers for my safety."

Amy and Brad will soon be married in a lovely beachside wedding, which Joan and Joe will proudly attend. Would such a storybook ending have occurred if my friends hadn't trusted? Was Amy saved from impending disaster because her grandparents decided not to worry but to pray? It surely beats me; there are no certainties in life or romance. But Joe and Joan—and Amy, too—will assure you that trust is a powerful weapon in a grandparent's arsenal, a true ally when stakes are high and options are limited. Trust isn't magic; it isn't superstition or spiritual naiveté. It is, they believe, a small, simple movement of the heart. Linked with love, it has power to shake the earth.

I don't know anyone who voluntarily seeks out situations that demand trust. Like a visit to the dentist, these experiences usually involve a level of physical and emotional distress that I, for one, would rather avoid. Unfortunately, being a grandparent doesn't grant me immunity from life's larger problems. As my family grows, as my children and their children attach themselves more securely to my heart, my own vulnerability increases. Unfailingly, new developments give me new reasons to trust.

When our daughter informed us that she and her husband were expecting their second child, a risky pregnancy because of her earlier premature delivery, it wasn't the only family headline to grab our attention. Within two weeks, our son announced that he and his wife were awaiting the birth of twins. These baby treasures, all due the same month, were at once a source of pride and a focus of concern for my husband and me. We stood on the back deck and hollered at the squirrels: "Three more grandkids!" Then we went inside and got on our knees.

Multiple births, it turns out, are not an obstetrician's favorite event. They bear more watching and careful oversight than regular pregnancies, said my doctor, himself a grandfather. Our daughter-in-law, just over five feet and barely one hundred pounds when not carrying babies, managed nicely with her firstborn, but twins meant a different set of rules.

"I wish someone had told me about this earlier," my daughter-in-law remarked after her father uncovered the existence of twin aunts Rosie Belle and Nellie Belle. "I don't think we'll be using those names." There was ample time to ponder alternatives. Our daughter-in-law was admitted to the hospital twenty-six weeks into her pregnancy and remained there on strict bedrest until she delivered the twins over two months later.

In the interim, two sets of grandparents scrambled to hold down the homefront and meet the demands of a busy toddler awaiting her siblings' arrival. Our son, off to work each day, took over the night shift and early morning duties, visiting his wife daily and taking his daughter to see Mommy on weekends. Meanwhile, their house was transformed into babyland central. A total of three cribs decorated the bedrooms, with a bassinet for backup in the parents' room. Rugs were tossed aside and easy-care hardwoods were installed. A guest room was outfitted for us visiting grandparents, who spent the night when our daytime responsibilities wrapped up. Painting and scrubbing, reorganizing and refurbishing, we were happily distracted from our worrisome thoughts. Busy with chores, we could trust that all was well, that the twins and their cousin-to-be were protected by the gentle force that had willed and welcomed their existence.

I'm glad no one could have told me about all of this in advance. In my limited experience, anticipation and expectation are worse than the actual event; watching and waiting are by far the hardest part of the process. But grandparents, I've found, are made of sturdy stuff. And when we're not feeling sturdy, we can always fall back on trust.

In September of 2001, my husband and I had gathered our family on an isolated island off the Florida panhandle to celebrate our thirty-fifth wedding anniversary. All of our children were with us, as well as our grandchildren and my folks, the esteemed great-grandparents. It was a memorable week, full of good talk and good food, baby laughter and grownup joy. Being with family was the best way to celebrate our marriage, we'd decided, and we were delighted that they had all arranged their overloaded schedules to join us.

Our days usually began with an early morning walk by the water while the kids were busy with breakfast. Then it was time to hit the beach or the pool, grab a fishing pole, or take a book and find some shade. On September 11 we were up and out early, quietly, so as not to disturb late sleepers. Coming back, we met our son who had been out running, earphones on his head, radio in hand. He gave us a hint of what was happening to the world as we knew it.

The sun continued to shine on the water outside as we huddled by the television that day and the days following. At night, under a glorious moon, our mealtimes seemed especially poignant. We took turns blessing our food and each other, recognizing the importance of being together, the gift of each other's presence, and the significance of the experience we had shared.

I don't know why we were fortunate enough to be gathered as a family, safely remote and protected, on the day our country was violated and our countrymen lost. I only know that I'm grateful to have been with those I love most in the world on the day I would most have worried about them. I had trusted that our vacation would bring us all closer, that it would give us ever more reason to value the comfort and security of family bonds. Well, it surely did. And my memory of September 11, overlaid as it is with sadness and grief, gives me even greater reason to trust.

---

*Grandparents aren't immune to worry or stress. As our families grow and expand, so do our cares and concerns. Trust is a reliable tool we can use to dispel fear and strengthen our spirit.*

## CHAPTER FIVE

# A Time to Serve

*SERVICE TO OTHERS*
*IS THE RENT YOU*
*PAY ON EARTH FOR*
*BEING HUMAN.*
  *Coretta Scott King*

Years ago, when I was young and naive, I used to dream that my husband and I would undertake noble, unselfish deeds as soon as our children were grown and on their own. We'd be a dynamite team, I was sure, building houses for the needy, serving soup to the hungry, traveling to exotic places where we'd right social wrongs and eliminate political injustices. Children of the sixties, we'd return to our radical roots, letting our hair grow long and wild, eating beans and veggies, selflessly sacrificing for the greater good. Together we'd challenge the system and make the world a better place than we'd found it.

Things haven't turned out exactly as I envisioned. When our kids eventually grew up and left home, our nest was as empty as a sandbox on a rainy day. The hallways echoed with the memory of their games and the refrigerator looked like it had lost its favorite customers. But the newly independent young adults who had finally vacated their bedrooms were still our kids. They continued to claim our hearts and a great deal of our attention. Sometimes they needed our help, sometimes just a listening ear or a shoulder to lean on.

We did our best to be available. If nothing else, we stayed busy. On one frenetic weekend, after renting an unsightly, underpowered yellow moving van, we cleared out the insides of a family lake house, installed one of our kids in a new apartment, and then transported another child's belongings across state lines into campus housing. Typically, we thought nothing of jumping in the car for a ten-hour drive to watch our daughter play soccer in a soggy fall rainstorm. Back then, we'd hustle three hours up the road just to hang shelving in a dorm room the size of a closet. Footloose and fancy-free though we appeared to be, family still came first. As empty nesters, we were relieved to discover that our lives weren't stagnant, but more full than ever.

When our children began marrying and having babies of their own, there were new reasons to be available. House projects and child-tending moved to the top of our list. As the family grew larger, our sphere of influence broadened and deepened. It was different than I'd expected, but kind of nice. Our kids needed us in new and grownup ways. We were their parents, but also their friends, good friends who could be counted on for counsel and support. Of course, we needed them as well. Their friendship was the best payoff parenthood had given us.

So far, our children and grandchildren haven't diverted us from saving the world. We don't use them as an excuse to bail out of social responsibilities, but still manage to commit time and what small talents we have to a number of worthy causes. On a scale of one to ten, however, family gets highest marks, ranking far ahead of any community outreach or volunteer opportunity that might claim our interest.

Somewhat reluctantly, I've accepted the fact that the eccentric, gray-haired hippie of my dreams will have to wait for another lifetime. The best contribution I can make to a broken, suffering world may well be the strength and support I can offer in the homes and hearts of my family.

My own parents have been remarkable role models. Their homegrown philosophy, "first things first," has been the guideline they've followed in making decisions and setting priorities since starting off as wartime newlyweds almost sixty years ago. Each time a new grandchild entered the world, my parents showed up ready and willing to take over. While we mamas were in bed recuperating, my mother turned out meals like a short order cook and tore through piles of laundry like it was her favorite leisure activity. While the new daddies were off at work, my father entertained older grandchildren and tackled never-ending repair jobs we'd all been too preoccupied to finish. Unfailingly, my folks could be counted on for at least one long weekend of babysitting every year, giving us harried young parents a few days of quiet romance away from the maddening crowd. And if an emergency arose or a special occasion presented itself, when a grandchild was ill or had an important football game to play, my mother and father cleared their calendar and made room for what they considered their most important responsibilities.

Today, their six children, twenty-two grandchildren, and growing cadre of great-grandchildren are still at the center of my parents' lives. They continue to serve as they've always done, by their loving presence and willingness to help. For their efforts, they've been blessed with the energy and spirit of people half their age, as well as the love and respect of their family. Veritable poster kids for the Fountain of Youth, their ability to focus on others instead of themselves, their desire to be useful, productive members of their family and community, has given them the healthy glow of the ever young.

All around me, I see other grandparents involved with their children and grandchildren in much the same way. It's not hard labor, just a firm movement forward when an extra hand is needed or a kindly presence required.

There's my neighbor around the corner, who happily strolls her grandbaby in the park while her daughter attends classes at a nearby college. And the devoted couple down the street who tote their grandson to summer camp each morning while his parents are at work. There's my friend Dottie Lou, who found herself at Disney World after agreeing to be temporary nanny for her delighted grandchildren. And my good neighbors across the way, who became part of their grandson's home-schooling curriculum when they taught him job skills and a sound work ethic at their place of business. There's my friend Janet, a single grandma whose grandkids keep her hopping from swim lessons to swim meets. And the caring folks at church who eagerly take over when chemotherapy leaves their daughter too fragile to manage their energetic young grandson.

Sometimes exhausting, always gratifying, grandparenting is a gift that enables ordinary people to do everyday things in extraordinary ways.

We've known our friends Anne and Ken since we headed south in the late sixties. They were among our first connections after a job transfer landed us hundreds of miles from our Yankee roots. Anne and Ken had relocated from Chicago a year or so earlier and had all the appealing qualities associated with Midwesterners. They were generous and self-effacing, modest and good-natured. We quickly sensed that they were the kind of people anyone would be grateful to count as friends.

It wasn't until many years later, however, when Anne and Ken had become grandparents, that the true depth of their character was revealed. Their first grandchild, son of their daughter Julie and her husband Frank, entered the world with a fighting spirit. From the first, Kenneth was loved and cherished. Born with a chromosomal deficiency that resulted in daunting physical and mental disabilities, he was nonetheless welcomed into his larger family with generosity and hope.

"We told Frank and Julie that they weren't alone in this, that we'd do whatever we could to help them," Anne remembers today. At the time, these new parents and grandparents had no idea what lay ahead. They only knew they were committed to facing the future together and tackling what needed to be done.

Doctors advised multiple surgeries to repair those parts of Kenneth's little body that had been affected by his genetic disorder. His cleft chin and palate alone required extensive hospital stays and follow-up therapy. When it was clear that Frank and Julie had to keep working to meet Kenneth's surging medical bills, Anne and Ken made the decision to revert to a single source of income. Anne left her job and became Kenneth's full-time caregiver.

"We took a step out in faith," she explained, noting that their decision was all the more significant because of Ken's chronic health problems, which could have made it difficult for him to continue working.

Kenneth's days at his grandparents' house began early, when their daughter dropped him off on the way to work. In the beginning, before his tiny mouth had been reshaped by delicate palate surgery, Kenneth was fed breast milk through a tube. Julie would leave a morning supply of milk at her parents' home, then stop by at lunchtime to pump more breast milk for the afternoon feedings. She usually picked Kenneth up around five, after which she and Frank would take over evening duties.

In addition to the routine of nourishing, diapering, and cuddling her new grandson, Anne faithfully brought Kenneth to his physical and occupational therapy sessions each week. Often, she'd meet her daughter there and together they'd learn songs, games, and activities aimed at stimulating Kenneth's growth and development. These they brought home and taught to the rest of the family, including Julie's three brothers, who unabashedly doted on Kenneth and took pride in his every accomplishment.

At the age of three, Kenneth was eligible for serious schooling. Taking advantage of a county program that encouraged early education for the mentally and physically challenged, Kenneth's parents arranged for him to board a bus at his grandparents' house each morning and return there each afternoon. Anne and Ken ordered their days so they could send their grandson off with a morning hug and greet him with a kiss when the bus brought him back in the afternoon. When not in school, Kenneth was Grandpa's boy, playing ball, taking walks, doing traditional things that forge unbreakable bonds between a grandfather and his grandson. Kenneth was a fixture at his Grandpa's company picnics, a favorite of Ken's fellow employees, an eager camera subject whose photo appeared often in corporate newsletters.

Kenneth is, perhaps, closer to his grandparents than many children, because Anne and Ken made an extra effort to interact with him as much and as often as they could. Now nearly a teenager, living halfway across the country from his grandparents with his younger brother Kyle and baby sister Bridget, Kenneth is a middle-schooler whose progress reflects the care and attention his family has showered on him.

"He's made great strides," his grandmother reports, adding that Kenneth's solo performance of "Take Me Out to the Ball Game" was the hit of his class concert. The song was Kenneth's favorite, she said, one he used to sing with his grandparents as they watched Harry Carey on TV leading the Cub fans in the traditional anthem of the seventh inning stretch. Outgoing and sociable, Kenneth is entering his teen years as he entered the world, with drive and determination.

Anne and Ken readily admit that, though they had no preconceived notion of what grandparenthood might entail, their intimate relationship with Kenneth and their over-whelming concern for him was a definite sur-prise. In their usual fashion, they are quick to suggest that, in similar circumstances, any grandparent would have done what they did. They feel fortunate to have had the freedom to lend a hand, to serve their family in a unique and significant way. But looking back, they're genuinely amazed that they could so quickly and easily step up to the plate when they were needed.

"We never thought we could do things like that," said Anne. "Things just happened and we did it." Perhaps it was grace that kept them going, they suggest, the peculiarly effective grace given to grandparents in real need of it. In the end, they say, Kenneth and the challenge he offered their family was a gift, one that made them all aware of how fragile life can be—and how rewarding.

Winnie and Gene live not far from Anne and Ken and are the same kind of generous, down-to-earth folks. When their daughter Mary and her husband Jim added little Kaitlin to the family, Winnie and Gene couldn't have been happier. Kaitlin was a winsome, talented girl, blessed with her mother's good humor and her father's musical abilities. Although Kaitlin's childhood was normal and active, her health suddenly became a serious concern when she was twelve. On a busy family weekend, when company was expected and Kaitlin wasn't feeling herself, she was brought to the pediatrician for treatment of what her parents suspected was a simple urinary tract infection. As it turned out, she was diagnosed with type 1 diabetes, a serious condition often misdiagnosed in children as flu, infection, or even stress. The news would dramatically change Kaitlin's life and the life of her family.

Simply put, Kaitlin's body doesn't produce enough insulin, a necessary ingredient the body needs to process glucose, the body's basic fuel. As yet, there's no cure for type 1 diabetes, but there is treatment, which consists of daily insulin injections to control blood sugar. Without them, Kaitlin would be unable to function properly and her organs would eventually deteriorate. Because their daughter requires constant monitoring and careful attention to diet and exercise, Mary and Jim quickly learned to measure Kaitlin's glucose levels and give her the correct dosage of insulin several times each day. Not to be left out of the loop, Kaitlin's grandparents decided that they should learn the technique as well.

Winnie and Gene were health-care neo-phytes, inept with a needle and distinctly uncomfortable at the thought of sticking such an instrument into their beloved granddaughter's tender skin. Nevertheless, they worked through their misgivings. In an emergency, they rea-soned, Kaitlin might need them to administer her insulin. Realistically, Mary and Jim might not always be around to dispense her medicine. Ultimately, my friends' overriding interest in their grandchild's health outweighed their fear. They enrolled in a private class with a compe-tent nurse, who instructed them in the mechan-ics of insertion and injection.

"We first practiced by torturing inanimate fruit," Winnie recalled with her usual dry wit. "We were given bottles of saline solution and some syringes and hydrated oranges to get the hang of it." The two medical trailblazers forged ahead, eventually graduating from uncom-plaining pieces of fruit to more voluble volun-teers. Kaitlin's parents were the last practice

targets before her grandparents were fully pre-
pared for their job. In the end, Winnie and Gene
judged themselves ready to give Kaitlin her
needed insulin.

"Mary and Jim will need breaks now more
than ever," said Winnie, whose confidence has
risen over time. "This is a constant, ongoing
demand, at least until Kaitlin's old enough to
do it herself."

Without a doubt, their ability to inject
insulin has been a big part of Winnie and
Gene's contribution to the family's peace of
mind. But their continued presence, their emotional strength, and readiness to listen have
meant even more, according to their daughter.
As Kaitlin gradually returns to an altered but
more normalized routine of school and sports,
she and her parents know they can count on
these courageous grandparents for unconditional support whenever and however it's
needed.

If such opportunities to serve draw us closer to our grandchildren, they also result in better relationships with our children and their
spouses. When we grandparents slap on an

apron or pick up a hammer, when we put a meal on the table or listen quietly to a loved one's concerns, we can't help but tighten the fragile threads that hold us all together. We stitch a wide, shiny binding around the edges of our family blanket.

Must we all be naturally unselfish, like so many of my friends, to qualify as successful grandparents? It certainly doesn't hurt, but it isn't required. Miraculously, grandparenthood seems to impose such virtues without any undue awareness on our part. It gently changes us from caterpillars into butterflies, transforming us into people we may hardly recognize as our own better selves.

Sid and Marilyn are retirees like my husband and me. Their time is their own, and they choose to spend a great deal of it with their family. They enjoy traveling, attending summer reunions at the beach, celebrating holidays with loved ones around them. They especially enjoy spending time with their grandchildren. And because their daughter-in-law has had serious health problems in recent years, they've had ample opportunity to do so.

Now Marilyn is a nurse and Sid a former traffic manager who deftly juggled the comings and goings of a sizable truck fleet. They each have talent and organizational ability to spare. But it isn't their special skills that make my friends a good fit for grandparental service. It's their generosity of spirit and willingness to help that allow them to smoothly transition into superstars. When their daughter-in-law's ongoing physical problems have been acute, when hospital stays and post-surgery confinement have restricted her ability to perform everyday tasks, Sid and Marilyn have stepped into the breach. They've washed dishes and fixed meals, taxied the kids to school and sporting events, kept the house tidy and raked the yard. Being available so their son could go to work each day and their daughter-in-law could mend, they've been a stabilizing influence on the entire family.

After another recent surgery, Sid and Marilyn alternated weeks staying at their son's home. "How's Marilyn?" I'd call to Sid as he passed our house on his usual morning walk. His response was predictable. It was Marilyn's week with the grandkids and she'd be back Friday evening. I'd meet Marilyn at the grocery store and we'd chat in the cereal aisle. "Sid's with the grandchildren," she'd report. "He's taking care of the kids this week."

During summer vacations, the grandchildren would regularly arrive at their grandparents' house for long, leisurely visits. "You'd love it," their grandson once confided to a friend. "All we do is play games and eat."

My friends tell me they find satisfaction in knowing they're able to help instead of sitting around like a couple of old retired folks "rocking and knitting." Being part of their grandchildren's life has been, for them, a privilege and a joy. "We're devoted to our grandchildren," Marilyn explained, "because we fell in love with them as soon as they were born."

Not every grandparent must rise to the level of sacrifice these friends of mine have had to face. Indeed, most of us grandparents have only limited chances, narrow windows of opportunity, to share our families' ups and downs, crises and difficulties. But whatever our circumstances might be, wherever our service may lead, don't mistake us for doormats. We're not martyrs or indentured servants. We're not slaves or simple-minded caretakers. We're the ones who freely show up with a ready smile, a sympathetic heart, a pair of hands eager to roll up our sleeves and get down to business. We're grandparents who, by a curious conjunction of circumstance, availability, and willingness, are uniquely fit to serve.

---

*Grandparents have opportunities to serve their families in unique and rewarding ways. In giving to my family, I realize my own significance in the unfolding adventure of family life.*

## CHAPTER SIX

# A Time to Limit

*NOBODY LOOKS LIKE*
*A GRANDMOTHER.*
*NOBODY FEELS LIKE*
*A GRANDFATHER.*
*BUT, READY OR NOT,*
*HERE COME OUR*
*GRANDCHILDREN.*

Lois Wyse

My former next-door neighbors and forever friends call themselves The Bad Grandparents. They're not really bad, of course. They're two of the most generous and caring people I know. My pals Barbara and David only insist that they're "bad" because they don't knock themselves out buying and spending for their grandkids. They've decided that these children have just about all the toys, clothes, games, and computers they could possibly require. Barbara and David don't wish to add to their material overload or frustrate themselves searching for the latest gizmos to occupy and entertain their grandchildren. They prefer to relax and enjoy the ride, effectively opting out of the dizzying cycle of kiddie consumerism.

I've always admired these so-called bad grandparents. They seem to have gotten it right. Grandparenting isn't about how much or how many, Barbara and David have discerned, but how deep and how true. Like avid treasure hunters, they search for ways to grandparent that involve time and activity rather than cash and carry. They show up for Little League games and clap like mad at spring dance recitals. They fill in on long weekends and baby-sit when business trips take parents out of town. They find pleasure in caring interaction rather than careless indulgence.

At their granddaughter's birthday party, Barbara and David were on hand when a petting zoo, complete with furry goats and braying donkeys, was imported for the celebration. "There were fifteen two-year-olds and pens of noisy animals," Barbara later reported. Though it was far beyond what these modest grandparents might have planned, they were there to pitch in and enjoy the occasion. In the end, they admitted, "We loved it," because it was one more opportunity to spend time with their grandchildren.

I've tried to apply my friends' balanced attitude to my own grandchildren. There might not be a menagerie in our backyard, but the kitchen is full of interesting oddities our littlest grandchildren can pull out when they visit: plastic Tupperware containers and noisy pot lids, shiny measuring spoons and soft woven potholders. We have a button box upstairs and a basket of favorite books, as well as crayons and coloring books for use on rainy days. For older grandkids there are wild birds to investigate, leaves to gather, parks to explore, shells to collect. Birthday gifts? How about savings bonds and books, pajamas and underwear? Selfishly, I want my grandchildren to like me because I'm fun to hang out with, not because I'm a good source for monster trucks and video games.

Like my friends, I too have learned that the art of grandparenting entails establishing and reviewing limits. In the honeymoon period, when grandchildren are but talcumed bundles of vulnerability and charm, there's little call for boundaries. You don't argue with a howling infant who wants something to eat at three in the morning. But as grandchildren outgrow their diapers and start viewing your antique coffee table as a racetrack for their Hot Wheels, the rules must inevitably change.

When my first grandchild reached that prickly plateau known as the much dreaded and often terrible twos, I found that I couldn't always be the nice guy. Little Ray was a handful of energy and independence, a sharp reminder of why I had children in my twenties. On a leisurely stroll to the local pier one sunny afternoon, we saw fishermen gathered and families delighting in the harbor view. Birds were soaring, the water was high.

"Hold my hand on the pier, honey," I counseled my grandson sweetly. Ray seemed agreeable enough as we climbed the pitted stone steps, inserting his little hand in mine like a tiny soldier following orders. We ambled down the long stretch of boardwalk to the pier's wider end, where pilot boats docked and tourists scanned the water for dolphin and turtles. Off to the side, a sun-weathered angler displayed a large shark he'd just reeled in. At the sight of the toothy fish, I instinctively clutched my grandson's hand more tightly, looking down to be sure he was still within grabbing distance. Alas, my concern was met with a ferocious pout, complete with furrowed brow and curled up lips. He'd had quite enough handholding for the day, Ray had decided. A battle was clearly brewing.

Picture if you will, a harried middle-aged woman in an oversized sun hat wrangling with a grumpy kid in short pants and flapping sandals. The lady in question desperately strives to maintain her dignity while the child tries as hard as he can to upset it. The duo appears to be dancing. A tango perhaps? The Mephisto Waltz? No, just an overwhelmed grandparent and a recalcitrant grandchild locked in a prenaptime tug-of-war.

People stop to stare. Elder oglers, grandparents no doubt, grin knowingly at each other like charter members of a secret club. Young parents grimace and pull their little charges out of the odd couple's careening path. *Prime candidates for the Cartoon Network*, their faces seem to say.

"You have to hold my hand when we're on the pier," I repeated firmly and a little impatiently to Ray. The formerly docile child who had turned strong and fierce with anger paid no heed. Doggedly twisting and writhing in my grasp, he moved over the wooden planks like a square dancer with a flame under his feet. His nimble fingers wiggled in mine like a fish on a hook. But I steadfastly refused to budge; the death grip I had on his little boy wrist remained tight and true. I knew my responsibility, after all; one false step and my precious grandson was shark bait. Ray didn't like my rules, but they kept him in the game.

Until then, I had been the fairy godmother, the fantasy grandparent, the Hollywood dowager entertaining every wish and whim. Maybe I wasn't living in reality, but I was happy. The battle of the boardwalk popped my bubble. After that, I knew there was no turning back. If I were to survive the era of grandparenting that loomed before me like an exciting but unfamiliar passage, I'd have to set some limits.

My friends Marlene and Frank had a similar awakening. As first-time grandparents, they were aglow with enthusiasm. Melissa was a darling, constantly changing, learning new things. Marlene and Frank would return from a visit with their granddaughter overflowing with Melissa stories, pictures, and pride. It was a shock for them to eventually learn that there were limits to their grandparental tolerance. Unfortunately, the crisis was all about Wickie.

Now Wickie is a little mop of a dog, a Lhasa apso who sits quite low to the ground. If you were looking for something soft and mobile to clean your floors, Wickie might do. On the other hand, if you were in the mood for some heavy housekeeping, Wickie could easily be mistaken for a dustball. Despite her canine eccentricities, Wickie is a sweetie pie, a family fixture, a beloved pet who's been treated kindly for all of her fifteen years. Now hobbled and diabetic, nearly deaf and completely blind in both of her cloudy blue eyes, Wickie was unprepared for her encounter with fourteen-month-old Melissa. As it happened, so were Melissa's grandparents.

"Melissa was petting Wickie with one hand. Then, when we weren't looking, out came this little pink and white sneaker making straight for Wickie's middle," Marlene explained, still shocked that her angel girl had a side that needed taming. "It wasn't a hard kick, just a sneaky little tap, but enough to make poor Wickie jump a foot in the air." Melissa, her grandparents noticed, was learning the ropes. "Every time she saw the dog she'd try it, then give us a coy little smile to jolly us up," said Marlene. "We had to tell her, 'Melissa, that's not nice. That's our doggie and we don't kick her.'"

If it's a shock when our babies start acting up, consider the possibilities when our grandchildren enter their preteens and teens. Our friends Bob and Paulette, grandparents of twin teenagers, have learned the value of firmness and clarity when it comes to setting limits. Michael and Ayla, poised on the cusp of young adulthood, know they're fortunate to have concerned grandparents who insist on learning where they go and what they do when they're visiting. During school holidays and summer vacations with Bob and Paulette, Michael and Ayla are offered lots of fun and freedom, along with reasonable guidelines they're expected to follow. If their grandparents' wishes aren't respected, they know there are consequences.

"Limits draw respect," said Paulette. "They don't have to like what we ask them to do, but when they're in our home they have to do it."

For the most part, Bob and Paulette's grandchildren abide by the rules of the house. Curfews are followed, courtesy shown. At dinnertime, Ayla offers to help with the cooking. Afterwards, she and her brother clear and scrape the dishes. When Michael, an avid skateboarder, politely asked if he could invite some new friends over to watch a video, Bob and Paulette agreed, but made sure each child had parental permission for the visit. "It was no trouble," said Paulette. "They all just sat on the sun porch and we brought them something to drink. We'd really rather have them here with us and know exactly where they are."

For these friends, who have blended two families and are proud to claim five children and nine grandchildren between them, boundaries flow naturally. There's not much difference between the rules they set for their grandchildren and the ones they enforced when they were raising their own children years ago. "Setting limits comes easily to me," Paulette admitted. "It's always come easily to Bob."

Housekeeping guidelines, for example, are straightforward and fair. "We don't pick up their things. We don't move things out of the way so they don't have to pick up after themselves," said Paulette. At the same time, "the kids make their beds each day, but leave their clothes all over the floor. We never say a word. Just close the door and let them live with it."

Balancing a healthy respect for teen independence with the onerous duties of the surrogate parent is delicate work and requires practice. But success is usually proportionate to how effectively grandparents combine boundary-setting with mega-doses of time and affection. "Thank you so much for taking us around," Michael said to his grandparents one day in a spontaneous burst of quiet gratitude. It was enough, Bob and Paulette tell me, to make all their efforts worthwhile.

At my age, I've decided there are certain things I cannot or will not do. I cannot eat broccoli. I will not ride a roller coaster. Scary movies are never on my must-see list. And despite kindly encouragement from my yoga instructor, I cannot touch my toes without bending my knees. After my grandchildren showed up, I also learned that I could not and would not allow them to land me in the hospital. I have rights and a responsibility to survive. To insure my mental and physical well-being, I've compiled a set of rules I carry around in my head and pull out when needed. Three basic reminders usually mean the difference between sanity and insanity:

1. Grandparents are valuable but breakable; handle with care.

2. Grandparents are fun but fragile; they need rest.

3. Grandparents are visitors; they don't live here.

It is, of course, up to me to follow the rules, not my grandchildren. If my adored granddaughter lands a baby smack on my face, it's my job to take her soft little hands in mine and gently caress the sore spot, whispering, "Love Mimi, nice Mimi." After all, who wants to explain that the darkening bruise on my cheek came from the heaven-sent toddler I'm constantly bragging about?

If my back goes out because I've let my grandson ride around on it all day like a dray horse driver, I can't blame the little guy. I'm the one who has to say "Enough!" and call it quits. When my eyes glaze over and my head begins to throb because I've read too many *Curious George* stories to my insatiable young audience, it's my responsibility to put their favorite monkey on the shelf until the following morning.

On some occasions, my grandchildren stay up later than I. While I begin yawning around seven-thirty, the kids might be good until ten. I require eight hours of bed rest a night, while they make up lost sleep with a couple of catnaps. Sometimes I collapse onto a nearby sofa after lunch, my legs begging for respite. For my grandchildren, peanut butter and jelly isn't a midday sedative, but a performance booster that promotes all manner of indoor and outdoor athletics. Setting realistic limits on how much down time I need, how much my body and brain can withstand, is entirely my decision.

And the rule of thumb about visiting? I say leave them wanting more. There's no need to overstay. Surely there'll be a next time, and we can play and sing and read again. Too much of anything, however wonderful and good, spoils the appetite. In the case of grandparents and grandchildren, limiting our time together leaves a pleasant pang in the heart that guarantees other joyful moments. Even in the case of grandparents sharing the same household with grandchildren, boundaries can be observed. When staying for extended periods of time with my own family—after childbirth, for example, when extra help was required—I've relished closing my bedroom door and enjoying some much needed privacy. No doubt the kids have been glad for the break as well.

Most grandparents will agree that surviving the joys and rigors of grandparenting means acknowledging our physical limitations and paring down the amount of space folks are allowed to take up in our heads. "If people are honest, they'll admit that it can be exhausting," says Diane, who swaps grandparenting vignettes and advice with me over clumps of clay at our local pottery studio. Knowing others face the same sort of energy drain that I do helps me accept the restrictions that time and age inevitably impose. Getting tired and feeling like I've had enough doesn't make me a bad grandparent. It just means I'm not supposed to abuse my body and brain. I have limits and so do my grandchildren. It's my job to respect them.

Of course, mistakes will be made, minds will be changed where boundaries are concerned. If we grandparents are truly wise, we'll admit when we've limited too much or too little. When appropriate, we'll accept the possibility that our choices might not have always been the right ones.

Many years ago, when my friend Anne and her four-year-old grandson were shopping together, her pride and joy spied a pair of shiny red Mary Janes that were just his cup of tea. In case you've forgotten, Mary Janes are the shiny patent leather shoes girls wore with their favorite Sunday dresses. They had narrow straps that buckled below the ankle and perky grosgrain bows that sat up around the toes. The shoes were usually sold in black patent leather. To have found a pair in red was a discovery of monumental proportion.

No doubt the red Mary Janes would have attracted any child, whatever the gender. Nevertheless, Anne was horrified to think that this small male person in her charge might return home in a pair of girlie shoes. They didn't fit her notion of what a well shod boy should pull on for a neighborhood game of hide and seek or a few rounds of touch football.

"Boys don't wear Mary Janes," she had told Russell unflinchingly. "We can't buy them for you." Not surprisingly, the little fellow was crestfallen. His tears broke his grandmother's heart. The shopping trip was over, its mood of happy camaraderie quickly overshadowed by a cloud of disappointment and regret.

Today, Anne says, she'd do things differently. "Oh, yes. I'd buy him those Mary Janes if I had a chance to do it over again. I wouldn't care what other people thought or said about it." Mellowed by humility, seasoned by the lessons life has taught her, Anne has tweaked her rule book. "When they really want something," she now believes, "that's what they need to have."

Anne and her grandson are still speaking. The saga of the red shoes is part of their shared history and an ongoing source of family entertainment. Despite Russell's disappointment and Anne's regret, their relationship wasn't irretrievably damaged by this one isolated event. Their connection has been overlaid with other, happier experiences that have more than made up for the loss of the red Mary Janes.

My grandson Ray and I are still good friends too. He's growing up and doesn't need to hold my hand on the pier any more, though sometimes he wants to. Setting loving limits on him and the other grandchildren I cherish is part of my role as a caring grandparent. Slowly and gently, I'm learning how to do this.

---

*Grandchildren need limits. Grandparents need limits. Limits define and enhance our very special relationship. With practice, I can decide what limits are appropriate for my grandchildren and me.*

## CHAPTER SEVEN

# A Time to Heal

*THE VERY FACT THAT YOU DON'T LOOK OR ACT OR FEEL LIKE THE GRANDPARENTS OF EVEN A GENERATION AGO DOES NOT MEAN THAT YOU ARE LESS, BUT THAT YOU ARE MORE—IN EFFECT, AN EVOLVED FORM OF GRANDPARENTS, PRIMED TO DO A BIGGER AND MORE CHALLENGING JOB THAN ANY GROUP BEFORE YOU.*
Arthur Kornhaber

There's a framed award in my laundry room that tells me I'm the World's Greatest Mom. Each of my children signed it and presented it to me on Mother's Day in 1995. Perhaps it was one of my better years. Perhaps my children have short memories. In any event, the award says it is given, "For being the perfect example for future mothers to follow." It also says, "We love you."

I can only look at this private piece of wall décor about once a week. It makes me weepy and the wash won't get done if I'm crying into the fabric softener. The only place I can keep the award is in the laundry room. It wouldn't work on the front door or in the living room. The kitchen is out and the dining room inappropriate. "People would talk. I'd get a swelled head," I tell my kids.

But the truth is that the award stays in the laundry room because I'm embarrassed. Maybe a little ashamed. I love the fact that my children think I'm a good mother; I probably did a decent enough job. But down in my toes, in the little recesses of my soul where the dark stuff hides, I know I wasn't always the best I could have been. There were times when I lost my temper and forgot my kids were just children. Times when I expected too much and gave too little, ignored their feelings and neglected their needs. I was very busy, you see, cleaning and cooking, ironing and shopping, driving all over town—soccer and ballet, school and church. Lots of times I emphasized the *doing* instead of the being, *choosing* things over people, projects over play. Sometimes it makes me blush to remember the foolish girl I once was, masquerading as a mother.

Grandparenting is my second chance. When the Good Fairy shook her starry wand and transformed me into a grandmother, I was given the magical power that comes with the role. It's not only the power to play in the mud with my grandkids, I've discovered. It's also the opportunity to roll in the grass with my children, to be with them in ways that show my heart has expanded with love for them as my ability to love has increased. I can't go back and relive lost moments, but I can surely take a crack at healing the places where I should have and could have done better.

Our granddaughter Nichola is a little rainbow child. With round blue eyes and strawberry blonde curls, soft creamy skin and cheeks that beg to be squeezed, she's any grandparent's dream girl. At seventeen months, Nichola was scheduled for ear tubes, tiny wonders of molded plastic placed in the eardrum when there's been a history of infection or hearing loss. The apparatus effectively drains and ventilates the middle ear, leaving it clear of bacteria and opening the ear so sound penetrates normally. Nichola's ear infections had been too numerous to count, hence the scheduled outpatient surgery. Twins were on the way and the last thing our son and his wife needed was an unhappy toddler suffering through sleepless nights and long, miserable days.

Because our son had tubes in his ears almost thirty years ago, my husband and I were familiar with the procedure. But while Nichola was slated for a brief, early morning visit to the surgeon, our son had stayed overnight in the hospital because he'd been unlucky enough to have his adenoids removed at the same time. I well remember crying inconsolably at the sight of our helpless little boy being wheeled off to the operating room. I also remember the small stuffed monkey we had bought as a reward for his youthful courage and valor. The monkey had been our son's official greeter when he returned from the operating room.

Nichola's circumstances were different, but more involved. Her pregnant mommy had been admitted to the hospital earlier that week with premature contractions and was on strict bedrest at the same time her little girl was due for tubes. Nichola's much needed surgery would have been difficult to reschedule.

"Don't feel you have to come up for this," our son assured us. "It's not a problem. I can handle it." I heard Nichola in the background, crowing and chattering. Obviously, her father was managing nicely. A capable, caring daddy, he was certainly up to the job of Mr. Mom. But this was clearly a chance for us to pitch in. Perhaps we needed to be there for ourselves, available not only for our granddaughter, but for our son as well. The thought of him battling early, big city traffic with a hungry baby in the back seat—no food or drink after midnight— pushed us over the edge. We packed our bags in record time and hit the interstate.

The following morning, driving to the hospital in the pre-dawn darkness, I knew we'd made the right decision. With our son at the wheel, my husband by his side, and me in the back seat with a surprisingly good-humored baby, we made our way to the outpatient facility. Along the way, we encouraged each other with thoughts that it would soon be over, that

Nichola wouldn't feel a thing; she'd be far more comfortable with her magical ear tubes, we told ourselves. Not much was said about us grandparents being along for the ride, but I sensed our son was comforted by our presence. I know I was comforted by his.

In the waiting room, while her daddy filled out paperwork, our granddaughter joined the other toddlers scampering around the floor like puppies in a play yard. We kept Nichola busy, distracting her from her empty tummy with songs and stories, listening closely as doctors and nurses explained what would happen next. When the moment came for Nichola to be taken into surgery, we sucked it up and faced the music. Her daddy carried her to the operating room and held her while light anesthesia was administered.

"She's out," he announced when he returned moments later. In less than fifteen minutes, Nichola was gently rolled, like a sleeping flower, into the recovery room. Her awakening, however, was neither gentle nor subdued. Someone had played a sneaky trick on her and her lamentations could be heard clear down the clinic corridors.

"Perfectly normal," the kindly nurse informed us as we scrambled to calm the patient. The return trip wasn't peaceful, but at least it was in the right direction. Not until Nichola was home, in her own bed, did sleep and quiet finally come. Her daddy's old brown monkey, favored companion in crisis and in calm, awaited her in the crib.

I'm not sure why this unplanned adventure was such a healing moment for me. I only know that I'm grateful to have been part of the action. Reliving something with my grandchild that I'd experienced years ago with my child was cathartic. I'd had a chance for a do-over, a repeat performance. Maybe this time I did it better. In reliving a difficult memory, I comforted myself as well as my child and grandchild.

Grandchildren like our Nichola are everybody's neutral turf. They're a pivot around which a family interacts, a unifying element in the fabric of family life. In-laws and outlaws, sisters and brothers, fun-lovers and fuddy-duddies can't help but be drawn into the circle of light that floats like a halo around a grandchild's head.

As a grandparent, it's my privilege to participate in their lives, and the lives of their families, in a unique and intimate way. My grandchildren are tiny stitches that keep me closely bound to my children and their spouses. Sharing love and concern for these little ones, our relationships grow stronger, our acceptance and appreciation of each other deepens. Like any family, we move through joy and sadness, hurt and reconciliation, loss and gain. By virtue of our status, we grandparents are active participants, movers and shakers, in the ongoing saga of family life.

Some grandparents, of course, are called upon to do more than others. Some grandparents have stepped in and assumed roles their children, either by choice or through circumstances beyond their control, have relinquished. Some grandparents, generously and unselfishly, have made sacrifices that have significantly altered their lives and the lives of their grandchildren.

In her colorful autobiography written several years before she died in 2002, Rosemary Clooney chronicled a childhood shadowed by the burden of absentee parents. Ms. Clooney's father was an alcoholic whose disease kept him distant and unavailable. Her mother sought every opportunity to work and travel apart from her three young children. For Rosemary, the talented child who later became the quintessential "Girl Singer," the closest thing to home was her grandmother's house.

There, in a modest rental overlooking the Ohio River, young Rosemary, along with her brother and sister, found welcome and comfort. They had no central heating, just a fireplace and a few potbellied stoves, but it was enough to keep them safe and warm. The kitchen linoleum might have curled up at the edges, but the front porch commanded a marvelous river view. And though the size of their lot was small, it accommodated a tidy backyard garden, where lush tomatoes grew side by side with cheerful snapdragons. Her grandmother loved that house, Ms. Clooney remembered in her book. "Best of all," wrote the famous songbird, "she loved us."

Things haven't changed dramatically since Rosemary Clooney was a child. Grandparents are still raising their grandchildren, healing their hurts, jumping in when parents aren't around to do the job. In fact, the number of grandparents caring for their grandkids has increased over time. The 2000 U.S. Census found over six percent of children under eighteen living in a household headed by a grandparent. That number represented a climb from the 1990 Census, which reported that five-and-a-half percent of all U.S. families lived in grandparent-headed homes. The 1980 and 1970 data showed that segment of the population to be under four percent.

The most recent census figures also indicate that some forty-two percent of the nearly six million grandparents living with a grandchild are primary caregivers. In other words, these grandparents, not the parents, are responsible for their grandchildren's basic needs. Such non-traditional domestic arrangements, according to census data, were found in virtually every socioeconomic and ethnic group.

AARP, also known as the American Association of Retired Persons, maintains a Grandparent Information Center that specifically targets and assists grandparents raising grandchildren. It also offers guidance to step-grandparents, to grandparents concerned about visitation rights, and to traditional grandparents seeking to play a positive role in their grandchildren's lives. In their newsletter, "Parenting Grandchildren," grandparents find information and referrals to local support groups.

"If you are a grandparent raising grandchildren, you are not alone," AARP suggests. If you're interested in forming or joining a support group through their organization, they advise, you'll find many others with similar experiences sharing their knowledge and hope. You'll also find a place to belong where the triumphs and rewards of raising grandchildren are celebrated, along with the challenges such a job inevitably involves.

Several friends have experienced these challenges and rewards. They have either raised their grandchildren in the past or are helping to raise them now. Turning a grandparent into a parent isn't easy, they agree, but dire circumstance is often a call to action. Financial insolvency, addiction, death, or disability are often part of the picture.

"Everybody needs somewhere they can call home," one friend tells me. "For my grandchildren, our place is home." She and her husband took charge of their two grandsons after divorce had split the family and neither parent was up to the job of tending the boys. Raising them through the difficult teen years and young adulthood, these hardworking seniors combined parental and grandparental roles, fulfilling the basic need every child has: to have someone he can rely on.

Other friends have recently taken over care of their granddaughters, offering them the chance to grow and thrive in a stable environment. Alcohol and drugs had gnawed at the security these children once knew in their parents' home. For them, their grandparents' house became a safe shelter where consistency and structure coexisted with love and concern. After establishing legal guardianship, my friends enrolled the children in local schools, shopped for clothes and classroom supplies, investigated bus routes and class schedules. Now they're up with the sun to fix breakfast and see their charges off for the day. When it rains, they're at the bus stop, umbrellas in hand. If a teacher spots a problem in the classroom, they're the ones called in for a parent conference.

"Just when I was getting ready to file for my Medicare card, I find myself raising grandchildren," my friend says with good humor. She's grateful for the chance to make a difference in her granddaughters' lives and for her husband's willingness to revisit parenthood along with her. "We're both committed to this. These children are a gift to us."

Caring for their grandchildren gives a focus to their lives and presents an unusual opportunity for teamwork. "It's taken away a lot of the pain" inflicted by addiction, they agree, allowing them to sleep through the night. "We have a peace we never dreamed we'd have. It's such a comfort to know we can do for our granddaughters what we're not able to do for our child."

No one plans to raise two sets of children. No one hopes to be a daily diaper-changer or prom chaperone at sixty. But the fact is that grandparents continue to fill the shoes of parents who are overwhelmed or unmotivated. The truth is that grandparents are often the only advocates and intermediaries a child may have. Even on the fringes of a family's fragile environment, grandparents can sense the gravity of a child's situation. When they take action to change that environment, miracles happen.

A dear friend of mine is a radiant, sun-dappled young woman. Her quiet confidence and gentle manner are soothing music in a cacophonous world. Not many would guess that she's the product of a topsy-turvy childhood, full of loss and pain. Her stability, she claims, can be traced directly to the years she spent with her grandparents.

"If I have any happy memories of my childhood, they're of my grandparents' house," she told me over lunch one day. "It's where my roots are." The youngest of seven children, she faced early rejection and abandonment: her father had left even before she was born. Her grandparents, especially her grandmother, took care of her each day while her mother worked to support their family. "Grandma didn't play with me. I entertained myself," my friend remembered. "But I felt safe just being around her."

Her family moved out of town when my friend was school age, but summers were always spent on her grandparents' farm. There she helped pick corn and peas and tended the chickens, falling back into the easy routine of rural life. As a teenager, the connection deepened despite geographical distance and continuing family stress. Following a suicide attempt when she was fifteen, my friend was institutionalized in a setting that allowed no visitors. Her grandparents had come to stay with her mother while she recuperated in the hospital, and through those long, desolate months, only one thing made the experience bearable. It was the sight of her grandmother, standing outside the hospital each day, waving up to her as she stared out the window of the psychiatric ward.

"It was a secret thing she'd do," said my friend, tears clouding her clear blue eyes. "There was a cemetery across the street from the building and she'd show up there faithfully. She'd bring my sister and my mother along too. It was the only way I got to see anyone." One day on her usual visit, her grandmother took the family dog, whose violent barking had summoned help for my friend when she was near death. "That little dog saved my life," she said. "I'll never forget Grandma holding him high above her head so I could see him through the window."

Today, my friend has grown beyond her past. The values she learned in her grandparents' home are the ones she's carried into adulthood. "I can't believe how well I turned out," my friend muses. "It's all because of my grandparents."

Grandparents aren't wonder workers. We're not magicians who can pull a rabbit out of a hat and make everyone smile. We don't have the power to change circumstances beyond our control. But we can make a difference. We can try. And in the process of our trying, we are ourselves transformed.

---

*Grandparents are givers and receivers of healing. In the unseen chambers of a grandparent's heart, gentle transformations and quiet miracles take place.*

# CHAPTER EIGHT

# A Time to Remember

*THE PRESENCE OF A GRANDPARENT CONFIRMS THAT PARENTS WERE, INDEED, LITTLE ONCE, TOO, AND THAT PEOPLE WHO ARE LITTLE CAN GROW TO BE BIG, CAN BECOME PARENTS, AND ONE DAY EVEN HAVE GRANDCHILDREN OF THEIR OWN. SO OFTEN WE THINK OF GRANDPARENTS AS BELONGING TO THE PAST; BUT IN THIS IMPORTANT WAY, GRANDPARENTS, FOR YOUNG CHILDREN, BELONG TO THE FUTURE.*

*Fred Rogers*

I met Anna Maria at a church carnival. The event was a typical fall fundraiser, with pony rides and games for the children, cookies and cakes lovingly baked by the women's guild, arts and crafts proudly displayed by local artisans. I came dressed as a clown, a scary thought made even more frightening by the fact that I had to operate a popcorn machine and twirl cotton candy in whiteface and wig. When Anna Maria showed up to help, I was more than ready to share my workload. I manned the popper while she took over the cotton candy concession.

Now cotton candy is a kid's fantasy meal. Light and airy, with gossamer strands shot through with irresistible clumps of hardened sugar, it melts in the mouth like a dream half-remembered. We had two colors, pink and blue, so the candy maker had to be a skilled sugar-spinner *and* have the ability to juggle two batches at once. Anna Maria was up to the job, however; her sticks of cotton candy were works of art. Like a sculptor with a magic chisel, she pushed an endless supply of paper cones round and around the whirring candy machine, mounding ordinary wisps of sugar into castles of confectionery delight.

Watching from my popcorn station, I was dumbstruck by Anna Maria's speed and confidence. As our line of patrons lengthened and demand stepped up, it became clear to me that she was no pretender to the cotton candy throne. At four-foot-nine, with hands as quick and nimble as a child's and eyes dancing with a merry sense of fun, she could easily have been transported from another time, another world.

"Where did you learn to make cotton candy like that?" I asked, tact losing ground to curiosity as my wonderment grew. "Oh, I was in the circus for years," Anna Maria said off-handedly. "During breaks, we'd work the cotton candy machines. It's not hard; it just takes practice."

I peppered her with more questions and she regaled me with tales of her life. Her parents had come to the States from northern Italy, eventually settling in Minnesota, where Anna Maria had grown up. She and her siblings were a lively bunch. With her sisters, she was part of dance troupe that entertained at carnivals and fairs. During a booking in Mississippi, she met her husband Don, whose large, colorful family quickly drew her into the excitement of circus life. Under Don's tutelage, Anna Maria became a full-time performer, traveling the country with the family's eye-popping acrobatic act and adding eight children of her own to the mix. Years later, after retiring from the big top, she and Don settled down on a six-acre coastal spread with a breathtaking marsh view.

"You'll have to come visit us some time soon," Anna Maria said as we broke down the machines the church had rented for the day. "It's an interesting place."

When I finally drove over to see my new friend, I realized there would always be surprises in store where Anna Maria and Don were concerned. Their modest home, well hidden behind a bustling main road, was literally surrounded by circus rides and games the couple had collected over a lifetime. There was a Ferris wheel, a merry-go-round, and a pint-sized train on a small track that was perfect for kiddie travel. There were gentle brown-eyed donkeys for little riders and a collection of old circus toys that could have graced the finest Manhattan antique store. A separate building held an intricate combination of model trains and tiny towns, metal grids and electric switches elaborate enough to beguile kids of all ages.

As I toured the grounds and inspected shelf after shelf of circus memorabilia, it occurred to me that my friends were historians of a sort. They might not qualify as museum curators, but they were certainly keepers of the flame. Anna Maria and Don had preserved their memories in an oversized, open-air album that was a remembrance of things past as well as a focus for present-day amusement.

"We hope to open it up as a place where children can come and have a good time," Anna Maria told me while Don petted Millie the docile donkey. For now, they said, it's adventure central for their sixteen grandchildren and four great-grandchildren, who are always welcome to investigate and explore.

Before I left, I roamed through a double-decker trailer Don had customized for use as the family's home away from home when he and his wife were on the circuit. It now holds a place of honor on their property, filled with aging black and white photographs, more old toys and children's books, and lots of happy memories. In the pictures, a younger Anna Maria looks smart and perky in shiny circus garb; Don is handsome and confident, striking a dramatic acrobatic pose. As they show me around, pointing out niches where the children slept and the family took their meals, my friends bask in the glow of yesterday.

Who can say if Don and Anna Maria would have begun their unusual collection had there not been children and grandchildren to share it with? Without family encumbrances, they may well have had more time and money to invest in their project. They might even have taken very real pleasure in constructing a backyard circus without the noisy distraction of children underfoot. But having kids around to enjoy and appreciate their efforts has enhanced and intensified their pleasure, my friends tell me.

"The grandchildren love it," they report. They visit often and sometimes spend the night, playing in the garden of their grandparents' memories for as long as they please. It's a chance for them to see a side of their grandparents they might not have fully understood. And it's an opportunity for Don and Anna Maria to remember the past with their grandchildren's encouragement and companionship.

Grandparents are blessed with the long view, the broad perspective. We've been around the block often enough to have a large store of material—if not in our backyards, at least in our heads and our hearts—that's worth sharing. Grandchildren make an ideal audience for our wanderings back in time. They're an admirable excuse to revisit where we've been, a reason to embrace and celebrate the past and to be grateful for its gifts.

My father readily admits he's no Mr. Fix-it. He can paint a mean wall and even refinish small pieces of furniture, but he modestly claims he's just patient and plodding, not necessarily handy. So when he began constructing small Christmas crèches as holiday gifts for our elementary school teachers years ago, we kids were duly impressed. Dad's rustic offerings won us major points in the classroom and kept him busy with hammer and nails while the rest of the world was racing around the shopping malls searching for presents.

For our first Christmas as a married couple, Dad made a crèche for my husband and me. It was just like the ones he'd made years before, maybe better. Dad hadn't lost his touch. The sturdy logs he had carefully hewn into short vertical pieces stood side by side on their plywood base. His neatly slanted roof, fashioned from a larger piece of rough wood, allowed a wide view of the stable interior. There we placed the solemn plaster figures of the new nativity set Mom had bought for us, along with a little bag of straw that made a nice soft bed for the miniature animals.

Dad's crèche stood the test of time; it grew up with our family. For more than thirty-five years, it's been the focal point of our annual holiday celebration. When our children were young, a visit to their grandfather's stable was always their first stop on Christmas morning, before pancakes and presents, phone calls and carols. In our house, everything played second fiddle to Papa's crib.

Of course, the crowd in front of our stable eventually grew smaller. As our kids left home and began their own holiday traditions, my husband and I continued to set up the manger, continued our annual Christmas morning visit. But we wished our family could share it still; it was too special a memory to lose. Clearly, the time had come to pass the torch. Our children and grandchildren needed stables of their own.

"Which wood was better, oak or pine?" my husband queried Dad as he set out to make stables for his children like the one their grandfather had made for us. "How thick was the plywood?"

With the old manger as prototype, my husband used spare weekends to craft the surprise gifts at his garage workbench. The finished products were simple and stately, a labor of love and remembrance. Following my mother's example, we included inexpensive nativity sets and bags of straw we'd tracked down at a local discount store. When we presented the clumsily wrapped packages to our kids that Christmas, we knew that, like our own stable, theirs would last for many years.

The stable-making tradition didn't stop there. When my parents visited my sister Mary Anne one recent Thanksgiving weekend, Dad was again pressed into service. Under his guidance, my brother-in-law Ed put together a Christmas manger for his son Brian and his new bride. Ed and Mary Anne aren't yet grandparents, but they know the grandchildren in their future will be part of an intergenerational tradition that's been handed down with care. Who knows who'll be next?

It's probably no surprise to anyone that finding these stables in our children's homes brings us immeasurable joy. Stopping by their houses over the holiday, the familiar sight of the stable in a front hall, on a dining room sideboard, nestled beside a lighted Christmas tree, helps my husband and I blend past and present. Seeing our grandchildren playing with the painted figures of the nativity tableau, we remember our own children fingering the angel and the cow, the little hay-box that did double duty as a crib. Watching my parents beside this latest generation of stables, their grandchildren and great-grandchildren around them, I'm grateful they're able to see that the tradition they began is valued and appreciated.

As I age, I find my memory isn't as reliable as it once was. I'm not always good with names and I might have a tough time remembering the title of that mystery novel I read last week. If I leave my grocery list on the kitchen counter when I go to the store, I invariably buy lots of food that's already in the cupboard and forget things I really need. I'm sure to panic if I don't park my car in the same spot each time I go to the mall and I spend more time and energy than I care to mention searching for eyeglasses that were in my hand just a moment ago.

Naturally, there are some things I'm happy to forget, but there are lots of things I wish I were better at remembering. Fortunately, I know, I have a special gift. As a grandparent, I can remember with my heart. I can remember with and through my grandchildren. And they can remember through me.

At the same time grandparents are remembering their past, savoring their memories, they're creating moments that their grandchildren will themselves someday cherish. Consciously or unconsciously, grandparents are transmitters of history, keepers of a larger heritage. The countless ways grandchildren honor their grandparents is proof of the impact grandparents inevitably make on little lives.

When I looked in my e-mail box about a year ago and found a message from Mootzann, I was ready to dump it in the desktop trash. I knew of no such animal and had learned over time that strange missives often mean weird viruses or salacious computer come-ons. Mootzann was certainly suspect. But in the subject line there was a name I immediately recognized: "from Ginna," it announced. There'd been only one person in my life with that name, a dear high-school friend I hadn't heard from in years. Ginna, whose middle name was Anne, had been short for Virginia. If it were the Ginna I knew, the one with a marvelous sense of silly and glorious wit, how could I miss the chance to reconnect? I held my breath and double-clicked to open.

Hooray! It was Ginna. She had found my e-mail address in an alumni magazine and had rushed to her computer to track me down. I wrote back and we quickly resumed our friendship through the wonder of the internet and the strength of early ties. After a few weeks of messaging, I was bold enough to inquire about her username. Mootzann had to be one of the strangest handles I'd come across in my admittedly limited computer experience.

"*Mootz* is Sicilian for cigar butt," Ginna e-mailed from her desk in New York City. "Isn't that dainty?" Her paternal grandfather, who was born in Sicily and came to Brooklyn while still a young man, used the nickname as a term of endearment for his grandchildren. He was

one of those aromatic, stogie-smoking grand-
pas, Ginna recalled. "It was a big honor to be
given the band from his cigar." When he landed in America, Ginna's grandfather dropped
the final *a* in his surname and traded in *Pietro*
for the less mellifluous but clearly Anglo, *Peter*.
He married a woman fifteen years his junior, a
legendary cook who fed their growing family
on his modest cobbler's wages as if they were
descendants of Italian royalty.

Ginna was only six when her grandfather
passed away at the age of ninety-five, but her
memories are vivid. When it came to choosing
an e-mail address, Mootz came to mind. There
was already a *Ginna*, the internet server had
informed her. There was even, to her surprise,
another *Mootz*. But, coupled with her middle
name, minus an expendable *e*, Mootzann was
uniquely her own.

"I know it sounds like a creature from a
1950 Japanese horror movie," said my friend,
"but it all just comes down to a connection to
my grandfather."

These connections, invisible links from one
generation to another, appear to have more

impact, more stability when they're forged between a grandparent and a grandchild. Like footsteps in fresh clay, they aren't easily dislodged or discarded. Time only enhances such memories of the heart.

A few years ago, we gave my Dad a memorial brick for his birthday. It was part of an effort to honor our local heroes and prettify our park. If you haven't heard of these clever campaigns, they're fundraisers with a punch. They raise money for refurbishing historic spaces and deteriorating buildings while recognizing folks who've done a good job of protecting and defending the rest of us.

A lonely stretch of grass overlooking the waters of our nearby sound needed sprucing up and our island Rotary Club decided to tackle the project. Their vision was a circular veterans' walk made from hundreds of engraved bricks surrounding a long-standing flagpole. The memorial space bordered our library and little theater as well as a public picnic area shaded by giant oaks and gnarly old cedars. It was a place that got a lot of traffic, a lot of visitors. A brick for Dad sounded like a good idea.

My sister and I and our husbands discussed the brick at length before the big purchase. "Do you think he'd really like something like that?" we asked ourselves. Dad was a low-key guy, not one to show off or blow his own horn. In the end, we'd decided, what the heck; all he can do is ignore it. Thankfully, he didn't. In fact, Dad's pleased as can be to show it to any and all comers.

The brick is simple, with his name and title on it. Dad was a Navy lieutenant and served in the Second World War. All my life I'd been listening to his naval stories, how he'd monitored German submarine activity off the U.S. coast and acted as patrol for American ships on their way to Europe. How he'd thrown supplies from his blimp onto waiting aircraft carriers below. I'd been born while Dad was on active duty and my mother, who had been living with my grandmother, sent him a lock of my bright red hair as a surprise. The war years were a big part of my father's life. The brick was a capsulized version of those years, a nod to his memory, a reason to be proud.

When his grandchildren come to see him, when great-grandchildren drag him to the park for a walk and a peek at the shrimp boats, Dad doesn't hesitate when asked about his brick. Sometimes we have to hunt for a while—there are so many, after all. But once we find the brick, read the inscription, and again assess its significance and value, the memories start to flow. For my family, the veterans' walk has meaning beyond its intent to acknowledge our local service men and women. For us it's a place where grandparents and grandchildren gather to share pieces of their lives, where past and present blend and become the future's happy memories.

Not far from the park, there's a small bistro where my husband and I love to lunch. Some mornings we'll stop for a bagel and coffee as well. Our friends Jerome and Tim, who own the café, are both committed to good food and good company in a relaxed, *al fresco* setting.

When they decided to revamp the menu and ratchet up the ambiance, Jerome and Tim chose to rename their establishment as well. Formerly known as The Village Bakery, it was rechristened Ruby Pearl's. The new sign now hangs jauntily outside, an art-deco design with a logo featuring a slender woman in high pointy heels balancing a tray of coffee mugs in one hand while her free hand hugs a hip.

"Ruby Pearl was my grandmother," Jerome explained. "Everybody loved her." When searching for names that had meaning as well as pizzazz, he said, hers surfaced as the perfect choice.

Closer to the beach, a new bed and breakfast draws visitors because of its commanding ocean view. A local builder opened it to the public and, after some months of operation, decided that afternoon tea might be a pleasant diversion for guests and locals alike. His grandmother was a longtime tea drinker who had shared the ritual of proper tea presentation with her children and grandchildren. The tea parlor, named in her honor, became Lucille's Tea by the Sea.

Lucille's daughter Anne, the owner's mother and my friend, is official hostess for the light teas that are solid enough to satisfy my husband's hearty appetite. Strawberry jam, Devonshire cream, lemon curd, finger sandwiches and "our famous scones" are among the treats we're offered. Do they taste better because they come straight from grandma's kitchen? Am I transported to a gentler, softer time when I pop a strawberry-laced scone in my mouth and immediately want another? Ah, yes.

I like to picture Miss Lucille gazing contentedly at the afternoon tea drinkers, smiling as her grandson opens the doors of his inn and invites friends inside. Surely she would recall the days when she served tea herself, cutting up lemons and baking delicate breads, enforcing rules of etiquette while indulging beloved children and grandchildren around her comfortable table.

I like to think about Ruby Pearl sitting comfortably at the café, watching the parade of people who stroll past her grandson's bistro. She'd love the croissants, and the special blend of iced tea served with orange slices. I feel sure she'd be happy knowing Jerome and Tim welcome guests with the same warmth she always extended to her own family and friends.

May our memories be as rich as the ones we find at Lucille's tea room and Ruby Pearl's cafe. May the moments we share with our grandchildren be as memorable as those these favored grandparents shared with theirs. May we remember—and be remembered—with gratitude and joy.

---

*Grandparents remember with and through their grandchildren. In turn, grandchildren remember with and through their grandparents. Together, we create new memories while honoring and celebrating the past.*

## CHAPTER NINE

# A Time to Love

*GRANDPARENTING IS*
*A VOCATION OF*
*LOVE.*

*Great-grandma Gigi*

Many of my friends became grandparents before me. When they did, I watched in consternation as these once mature, clear-headed adults turned into absent-minded chuckleheads. On social occasions, they'd use any excuse to rattle on about their grandchildren. According to my friends, these kids were far above the norm, exceeding the bar in everything from brains to looks to personality. As I yawned and tried in vain to change the subject, they'd press on unmercifully, displaying recent family photos and pointing out the latest grandchild's uncanny resemblance to themselves.

Rarely available for dinner or a movie, my former playmates could instead be found racing for whatever outbound plane, train, or automobile would whisk them off to their grandchildren's side. Global warming, tainted water supplies, election year politics, or polluted air were not the concern of these starry-eyed optimists. Their preoccupation with the sandbox set fogged their glasses and clouded their brains. Though I didn't understand it, I finally accepted the fact that, for these people, grandchildren came first. The rest of the world could wait.

Today, I think I might have been a little hard on my friends. I may have been a little too quick to judge what I deemed to be their aberrant behavior. Because I now jump like a lackey when a small child cries "Mimi!" and have been known to flaunt pictures of my grandchildren in supermarket checkout lines, I have a clear sense of what was ailing these folks who had preceded me into the hallowed halls of grandparenthood. I now realize they had fallen truly, madly, deeply in love.

I know this because I, too, fell head over heels for my grandkids. It wasn't a conscious decision on my part, any more than it was for my friends. Like awakening to find sunshine pouring through a window after an all night downpour, it was an unexpected gift. I hadn't known it would be so natural and spontaneous, so worthy of my attention. In my mind, grandparenting had been a daunting possibility. My bones were still aching from raising my own four children. Thoughts of babies on my hip turned my knees to jelly. But my fears vanished in the initial rosy moments spent with my first grandchild. There was no time to mull things over or change my mind. I was hooked like a trout on a line.

I love my grandchildren. I don't always like them, but I always love them. Sometimes they drive me crazy. They can be impertinent and obstinate, whiny and fresh. They can push my buttons and pull my strings. They might even try to manipulate me. But they are—each one of them—special presents, small jewels to be cherished and kept safe.

On a bad day, they'll jump on the furniture and refuse to eat. They'll run their dirty feet along the wall and poke me in the eye. Sometimes they'll even tell me I'm no longer their friend. But even on a bad day, when it seems like the rain will never stop and they're getting on my last raw nerve, they'll surprise me with a quick kiss or jolly giggle and turn me inside out. And on a good day, when the sun is shining and puffy white clouds are dancing across the sky, when they're sweet and smiley and eat every last bit of their oatmeal and applesauce, there's nobody else like them.

Erma Bombeck, the beloved Dayton housewife whose syndicated humor columns delighted readers until her death in 1996, once wrote an essay about her children that I found touching and true. The column addressed the fact that each of Mrs. Bombeck's children was her very favorite child. The firstborn was her favorite because he was the oldest, the second child because he was the one in the middle, the last was a favorite because he was the youngest of the brood. Every child was unique, with individual gifts and personalities that endeared that child to his mother. She loved each one best because of the special claim he made on her heart. The piece effectively put the lie to the age-old concern that someone older, younger, or more talented than oneself is the family favorite.

I read this column one Mother's Day and was touched that someone of Erma Bombeck's stature would express sentiments so near to my own. After the birth of my first child, I wondered how I'd ever love another as much as I loved him. When I became pregnant with our second, I approached my mother with the dilemma.

"You had six," I pointed out. "What happens when the others begin to arrive?" I assumed motherhood was a tightly lidded box that could only fit so many tiny treasures and no more. In my case, the box was small and held one curly-headed, blue-eyed baby boy. Thankfully, my mother assured me that a parent's heart is a remarkable muscle. "It expands and enlarges to include more children in a widening circle of love," she told me with a parent's wisdom and a poet's grace.

Her words sounded good, but I wasn't convinced until our second child arrived. Can you believe that he, too, was the perfect baby? His soft brown eyes, happy-go-lucky personality, and infectious laugh immediately made him my very favorite child. When baby number three came along, the potential of my heartstrings to stretch without breaking began to amaze me. My heart had become big enough. It could hold all the tender feelings I had for this beautiful, doe-eyed little girl who was now my favorite child, as well as my love for the other favorites in my nest. And baby number four, the one the nurse described as a delicate Dresden doll? Well, of course she became my favorite too. How could I help but tuck her into my heart and love her best when she filled me with such delight and happiness? She joined the rest of my children—each one my very favorite—who still make my life the fullest it can be.

"Grandchildren are the closest thing to having your own children back again," my friend Faye told me after she had become a grandmother. As I feed and bathe, burp and diaper my grandchildren, when we draw and dance and play in the park, I'm certain my friend was right. Just like my children, I love each one best. And just as my children are different, like colors in a rainbow with distinct and subtle hues, each of my grandchildren is unique as well. Today I embrace their individuality with unconditional love, celebrating the qualities that make them the special creations they are.

Most grandchildren have the benefit of knowing their grandparents after we've been through a bit of life. Like pebbles washed and rolled in a riverbed, we're rounder, smoother, easier to hold than we were before. On our best days, we're more lovable, more apt to show affection and care to those around us. We've been softened and mellowed, sculpted to fit comfortably into our grandchildren's world. Some of our most generous acts of love are quiet expressions of our enlarged hearts.

My niece Megan was recently married. Her husband Matt is from Tennessee and he and his family drove to Connecticut for the nuptials. At the rehearsal dinner, both families mixed and mingled—chatting, swapping stories, reflecting on the many virtues of the bride and groom. Matt's grandfather David was in attendance, a tall, wiry man with gray hair and an easy smile. He was tired from the long drive, he admitted, but very glad to be included. I was touched by his sincerity and warmth. Engaging and friendly, he was ready to participate in the celebration in his own gentle way.

At church the next day, David sat up front with his family. Ramrod straight, handsome in his dark suit and crisp white shirt, he was an attractive addition to the groom's side of the aisle. The day had been overcast and rainy, but the sun broke through just in time and the church was bathed in soft afternoon light. It fell on us like a blessing.

Later, at the reception, we enjoyed music, food and fellowship together. At each table, tiny silver-monogrammed boxes had been artfully arranged by each place card. After dinner and a few twirls around the dance floor, I opened my box, unraveling the intricate cardboard closure that served as a bow. Inside was a collection of cappuccino-coated almonds. "Matt's grandpa made the candy himself," a fellow guest whispered as I savored the sweets. They were, in a word, yummy.

Now there were probably close to one hundred people at that wedding. If there were even just five candies in each box, it meant that David had taken the time to put together five hundred of these tasty little treats. That was, I knew, far beyond what I'd ever consider hatching in my own humble kitchen. But then again, my grandchild wasn't the one getting married.

"So, did you really make all those wonderful candies we had yesterday?" I asked David at brunch the next day. We had gathered at my brother's house to round out the weekend events and were enjoying a mild, blue-skied New England morning on the deck. David modestly admitted his contribution to the celebration, remarking that hauling them in coolers from Tennessee was far and away the hardest part of the process.

Confectionery had been his lifelong hobby, he told me, and he was happy to give Matt and Megan something special he had created himself. As we spoke, a cake appeared in the background, laden with candles and rich creamy icing that tempted us all. It was David's birthday, his eighty-first. We sang the traditional anthem and wished him well.

Back home after the wedding, I enjoyed seeing the photos Megan and Matt sent over the internet. There were pictures of the happy bride and groom, a shot of my husband and me boogying like bobby-soxers, candid family stills that made us laugh and remember. David was in the pictures too, posing with his son and grandson, with his daughter and with the effervescent bride, who had obviously captured his heart. There were no pictures of David on the dance floor. He'd declined invitations from all the pretty ladies who'd asked. His legs were giving him a little trouble, he had said with a gentlemanly thank-you.

Six weeks after the wedding, we learned that David had died. "In the pictures, he looked terrific," my sister-in-law Fran said later. "No one would have guessed he was so ill." David's troubles with his legs were clots that needed immediate treatment upon his return to Tennessee. Sadly, an advanced cancer was also discovered and he never came home from the hospital. "The whole family was so glad he had felt well enough to attend the wedding," Fran told me. "He was an important part of the day."

I won't soon forget David or the generosity he showed to his grandson and bride. The vision of this faithful grandfather at work in his southern kitchen, lovingly preparing wedding chocolates, is a reminder to me that love thrives even when age and ailments threaten.

My niece Megan won't forget David either. "He made me feel very loved, as if I'd always been in the family," she said. "I'll always remember the wonderful hug he gave me the first time we met and the way he adapted so many of his recipes because of my allergy to peanuts and pecans." David had shared many stories of his beloved wife with her, Megan recalled. Best of all, he had confided to his grandson that he knew Matt would be as happy with his sweet New England bride as he had been with his own wife.

My brief acquaintance with David shows me that unconditional love has space and time to grow in the open, grassy field where a grandparent meets a grandchild. It's a love that is nurturing, life-giving, mutual. Grandparents and grandchildren flourish in the sunshine and fresh air they receive from one other.

Two grandparents I recently met through a mutual friend left an idyllic life in the dry and sunny southern California desert just to experience this kind of love. "It was awful to be so far away after our grandbaby was born," said Grandma. "We couldn't get here fast enough." The couple had been retired only a few months when they moved to the East Coast and became full-time caregivers for their daughter's eleven-month-old son. "I was ready to come," Grandpa admitted. Despite a lifetime on the West Coast, he is uncomplaining about the heat, humidity, and pesky mosquitoes that awaited him in his new locale. "You get acclimated," he said with an easy grin. "I'm not afraid of change."

Today, this generous couple thrives on the affection they receive from the towheaded two-year-old who shows up on their doorstep each morning ready to rumble. "The best part is being with him all the time," Grandma beamed, "receiving all the love he gives us each day." For her husband, time spent with his grandson is pure pleasure. "With our children, I was working, balancing a lot of things at the same time. Now I have plenty of time and there's no balancing act anymore. I can just enjoy him."

It's a big payoff for two people who had wondered if they'd ever have any grandchildren at all. Their daughter, a warmhearted, well-educated professional, formally announced her status as a gay woman when she was in her early twenties.

"It was a big relief," said her mother, for whom the revelation came as neither a surprise nor a disappointment. "Then she could be herself." Both parents were supportive and encouraging of their daughter, openly addressing her orientation with close friends and family. "Though it was hard at first, I wanted to let people know because it made it easier all around," her mother said. "We wanted to be as open as possible." Her husband agreed. "We never hid it. People knew right where we stood," he said. "Maybe they didn't understand, but they accepted."

When their daughter had been in a stable, committed relationship with another woman for nine years and had decided to include a child in their family unit, these grandparents couldn't have been happier. Because they had unconditionally embraced their daughter, welcoming a baby came naturally. "Our feeling was, how soon can you have it?" said Grandpa. "In today's families, after all, how many children are raised by single parents, or grandparents, or great-grandparents?"

"We were totally ready for a grandchild," said his wife, proudly displaying the latest

Halloween costume she had sewn for her favorite toddler. "Last year he was a bumblebee. This year he's Captain Hook." Their living room is filled with a mix of comfortable antiques and little boy books, grown-up collectibles and random toys. A highchair is standard equipment in the kitchen; a special bed has been designated for afternoon naps. "His naptime saves us," says Grandma, who manages to rest each day when her grandson goes down. Another scheduled break is a mother's morning out program at a local church, which he attends two days each week.

Both grandparents are upbeat and optimistic, but realists as well. "This is not the norm," Grandma says of their child-friendly routine, which takes its toll on older bones and virtually precludes any spur-of-the-moment plans. They understand that as school-age years approach, their grandson may face questions, teasing, and perhaps prejudice from those who might question his non-traditional family structure. "There will be some rough times ahead," his grandmother expects, but the presence and support of two devoted grandparents will make a difference. "With us here we can get through these issues," his grandfather is certain. "He's found his island of safety with us."

Meanwhile, these likable folks are focused on the present and the joy each moment brings. If beds are unmade or dishes left undone, they're not worried; tomorrow is another day. If something is broken by a pair of small, slippery hands, it's easily mended or duplicated. "They're just material things, not like memories that can never be replaced," says Grandpa. It's completely different from rearing one's own children, his wife has found. "I'm more relaxed, more easygoing. It makes me want to go back and raise my children all over again," she said.

When people ask how they're able to do what they do, these grandparents are quick to insist that they're the ones who've been blessed, the ones whose lives have been enriched. "We're very lucky to be doing this," Grandma says. "Being a grandparent is the best possible job."

Seeing these grandparents in action is like watching the plot of a movie slowly unfold. It's an adventure flick, to be sure, maybe even a cartoon at times. It's a family drama, with a flaxen-headed youngster who steals your heart, a biography that makes you marvel at the depth of human resiliency. But the real thread running through the whole story is one of heady romance. The gushy stuff. It's the chemistry between two people whose love makes all things possible. Because of their commitment to each other, these grandparents can act as a team, slaying dragons and climbing mountains others might find too steep. Their married love, experienced first as husband and wife, then as mother and father, ultimately as grandparents, lightens their hearts, strengthens their resolve. They are heroes, pure and simple. They are lovers in the best sense of the word.

For me, falling in love with my grandchildren means falling in love with my husband all over again. Seeing him with a trio of granddaughters googling on his lap, watching him explain the finer points of pitching to his grandsons, I know how lucky I am to have married a man both gentle and strong. Having grandchildren also allows me to appreciate my children in a new way. Watching them artfully parent their children, seeing them interact as doting aunts and uncles, gives me a fresh look at their sensitivity, goodness, and faithfulness. If they weren't my children, I'd want them as friends.

An eighty-year-old grandmother of twelve recently sent me a poem by an unknown author that captured the essence of a grandparent's heart. The poem described a parent's love as passionate, deep, and free, strong and sure in the face of anguish or joy, happiness or grief. It described a grandparent's love—"the love I bear my child's child"—as a different emotion: softer, gentler, like rain falling on flowers, or wind blowing quietly through blossoming trees. When a grandparent lovingly embraces a grandchild, the poem concludes, "It's springtime come again."

I'm astounded to find that as my knees weaken and my eyelids droop, as my skin dries up and my head forgets where my fingers put last night's newspaper, spring is nevertheless blooming in my heart. Without a doubt, I'm growing younger on the inside. Things are simpler, clearer, easier to comprehend. Puzzles are solved, questions are answered. Surely, it's love that makes it so. And surely, my grandchildren are a vital part of this mysterious process. They are, you see, so very easy to love.

*G*randparents become unconditional lovers because we can't help ourselves. We're smitten with our grandchildren, bearers of love, companions on our journey, who lavish us with affection and affirmation. They call us to give it all back—to themselves, to others, to the waiting world.

## CHAPTER TEN

# A Time to Dance

WE ARE INVITED TO
FORGET OURSELVES
ON PURPOSE,
CAST OUR AWFUL
SOLEMNITY TO THE
WINDS
AND JOIN IN THE
GENERAL DANCE.

*Thomas Merton*

Our three young grandchildren and their parents had been with us two days when I rolled over in bed one morning, groaned at my aching back, and asked my drowsing husband,

"Where am I?" "You're on Mars," he replied, deadpan, then added sleepily, "So am I."

Growing older is a walk on the wild side. As my body retreats before the armies of time, my spirit, clad in youthful armor, advances like a bold warrior. My mirror tells me I'm over the hill, but my head insists I'm just vaulting the rainbow. As we age, some of our parts tire and weaken. Yet other parts continue to grow, coming to life as never before. Exercise and the ubiquitous balanced diet, blood pressure pills and vitamin E may contribute to a healthy lifestyle, but tending to my spiritual and emotional needs is just as important. I've cut back on red meat and upped my calcium dosage, but I've also found it beneficial to fortify my inner self with regular injections of my grandchildren's laughter. The endorphin rush they administer is sensible medicine. The warm fuzzies I feel when they're around boost my serotonin levels and pump up my serenity.

Even academia recognizes the importance of such emotional maintenance. A twenty-five year study begun in 1975 and funded by the National Institute on Aging found that people with positive views about growing older live longer. Conversely, negative images of aging can have significant health consequences, sometimes affecting the will to live. People whose self-esteem doesn't shatter when they discover another wrinkle on their forehead tend to outlast more negative minded seniors by a median total of seven and a half years, the study revealed. Moreover, these added years are larger gains than those made by giving up cigarettes, exercising regularly, or keeping the bad cholesterol count down.

"There's nothing we can do about aging," Suzanne Kunkel, co-author of the study and director of the Scripps Gerontology Center of Miami University in Ohio, said in an Associated Press interview after the study was released. "It's like sitting in traffic when you're late." You can either stress out and get upset, or relax, turn on the car radio, and think about how you'll deal with the consequences of a late arrival.

Fortunately, grandchildren are positive influences on a grandparent's self-esteem. They foster a desire to go on living and confer an enhanced sense of self-worth. Active, involved grandparents are usually having too much fun to be morose. When a grandchild races into a grandparent's arms, claiming attention, affection, and a break from life's serious side, can that grandparent feel he's anything less than wanted and loved?

My friend Pat was one of the best grandparents I've ever known. When she died quietly in her sleep not long ago, she left not only a host of bereaved friends but also a crew of grandchildren whose lives became lonelier without her.

Pat and her husband Harry were always quick to answer the call when their children or grandchildren needed them. Nothing was more important than their weekend dinners, where festive homemade meals were regularly served to their rapidly growing family. When our daughter was being married and we needed a couple of able-bodied guests to keep an eye on our grandchild during the wedding ceremony, it was Pat and Harry we tapped. They were naturals, and their generosity could always be counted on.

Pat was an avid exerciser. She generally popped in a video each morning and sweated to the regulation moves the skinny cheerleader on the screen demanded. She also watched what she ate, choosing a salad instead of a sandwich, unsweetened tea instead of the sugary kind. When we lunched together, my plate looked overfull in comparison to hers. Yet despite her vigilance, Pat always managed to keep a few extra pounds in reserve. They settled in her tummy and she routinely complained that she couldn't get rid of them.

"But you know," she'd tell me after once more lamenting her struggle with the scale, "I really have a great lap for grandchildren. It's soft and cushiony and just right for them to sit on. I guess it's not so bad after all. It makes me feel like a real grandma."

Pat's positive attitude and endearing self-acceptance continue to inspire me today. If I take myself too seriously or become too self-critical, if I lament the loss of my girlish figure and deride those laugh lines crinkling the corners of my eyes, Pat's memory erupts in my head, reminding me to be less self-conscious and more accepting of the passing years. If my grandchildren find some comfort in my mellowing body, I'll take it as a sign that the downside of aging has some built-in benefits.

Historically, grandparents like Pat and Harry have been honored and revered. With their gifts and experience, their bounty of love and unselfishness, grandparents have always played a significant role within their families and in society at large. Grandparents soften the edges, quiet the fray. They are peacemakers and healers, menders and nurturers. Native American, African, and Oriental cultures, as well as most European societies, have acknowledged the value added by an older generation. In the face of daunting geography and distracting social upheaval, even fast-paced Americans scramble to keep their ties to grandparents alive and meaningful. As the world of the third millennium unfolds, grandparents may well be more important than ever.

Meanwhile, the stereotypical grandparent is a vanishing breed. Instead, grandparents are showing up in all shapes and sizes, all ages and attitudes. We're working or retired, homebound or traversing the globe. We're jogging and golfing, windsurfing and running marathons. We're creating treasures at our basement workbenches, making art in sunlit studios. We're teaching and learning, finding new reasons to be alive and curious. Venturing out in stylish suits, comfortably clad in jeans and "I Love My Grandchildren" sweatshirts, our differences add flavor to the mix. Our common thread—unbridled love for our grandchildren—doesn't detract from the freedom to be ourselves.

Grandparents today can decide for themselves what type of role they'll play in the lives of their grandchildren: playful and friendly, relaxed and carefree, gentle but firm. They can even take a hands-off approach—distant but loving, observers of sorts—though this doesn't sound like much fun. As a grandparent, I'm the star of my own movie, the hero of my personal drama, the fascinating subject of my own song. In the presence of my grandchildren, I can be myself as never before. Their love and acceptance is heady applause reverberating in my ears.

"I love being a grandparent. I love everything about it," a friend confided fresh from a visit with her grandchildren one summer day. "Maybe it's because I know I'm a better grandparent than I was a parent." This friend packs spur-of-the-moment picnics and heads to the beach with her grandkids whenever weather permits. She sews dolly clothes for her grand-daughters and welcomes them to her farm. She knows it's time to break free of old constraints and be who she is. Her grandchildren love her for it.

There's good reason why the word "grand" is a key part of grandparenting. Being a grand-parent is a cause for joy, an invitation to cele-brate. Few grandparents find themselves frowning in the presence of their grandchil-dren. They're seldom glum when a grandchild is around. Grandparenting is a true vocation, a call to lightheartedness and blessed fun. With practice and perseverance, grandparents can become really good at what they do.

Years ago, whenever my parents planned a get together with their grandchildren, it was their custom to travel with a treat bag. The bag was a mystery sack, overlarge and bulging with things a parent might hesitate to pur-chase—candy and bubble gum, jacks and paint boxes, funny hats. Most of the stuff my father had found in the chaotic mix of shops and pushcarts on Vesey Street in New York City. He loved pawing through the bargain bins at lunchtime to find items he thought would delight his grandchildren. When the treat bag surfaced, chock full of goodies, the grandkids knew it was showtime: a trick was required before the treat.

With twenty-two grandchildren, my folks were understandably in store for lots of entertainment. They were the perfect audience, since nothing their grandchildren did ever got the proverbial hook. One time our sons did a juggling act. Another day the girls sang a duet. I remember that harmonicas often surfaced. And I distinctly recall the ear-bending tones of a nose harp. The quality of the performance didn't really matter; it was the willingness of the kids to put on a show that made their grandparents happy. My parents' peals of laughter, barely suppressed guffaws, and tears of joy revealed their secret motivation. They knew how to have a good time with their grandchildren and sought out every opportunity for fun.

Our friends Jane and Joel have a good time too. Each summer, they invite their children and grandchildren to the shore for a week of togetherness. There they spread the family into three comfortable condominiums and leisurely catch up on the latest family doings. Jane and

Joel's place is food central, they tell me, a revolving door with grandchildren coming in and out all day. It's a good arrangement because they're never far from the action and get to spend lots of down time with the kids. One year, when one of the grandchildren appeared to be lost, his grandmother turned out to be the missing link.

"They were searching for him all over the beach," Joel related. "It was more than an hour before they found him. His mother was going crazy." Where did the happy wanderer show up? Watching television with Grandma, in the peace and quiet of her room. While frenzied aunts and uncles, parents and cousins scanned the water and canvassed the beach, their grandson was kicking back, hanging out, enjoying time with his grandmother, far from the noonday sun.

"He came up to get a snack and stayed to rest with me," Jane explained, barely suppressing a giggle. She regretted her family's distress but found the incident mildly amusing. "We never knew there was a search party out for him. They were ready to call the police." Once again, one of her grandchildren had been an ally in play, a secret comrade. She couldn't feel much remorse about that.

The bonds that keep us tightly attached to our grandchildren are now officially celebrated in the United States. Marian McQuade, a West Virginia housewife who hoped to draw attention to lonely nursing home residents and encourage grandchildren to mine the rich heritage and wisdom of their elders, originated the idea of a special day dedicated to grandparents. In 1978, President Jimmy Carter, in a tip of the hat to his forebears, proclaimed that National Grandparents Day would be observed on the first Sunday after Labor Day each year. Today, Mrs. McQuade's descendants carry on her work through the National Grandparents Day Council, a non-profit corporation that works to enhance the holiday by supporting intergenerational activities all year long.

When Grandparents Day comes around every September, expensive cards with soft, flowery sentiments appear in corner card shops. Hometown newspapers run heart-tugging pictures of fourth grade girls eating pizza with Grandpa in the school cafeteria. Slowly, Grandparents Day is evolving, gaining status and respect, much like Mother's and Father's Day. It may be just another savvy marketing tool for flower shops and greeting card companies, but it touches me nevertheless.

My dear friend Rita, great-aunt to her niece's daughters Madeline and Sarah, isn't a grandma in the technical sense, but is an especially caring surrogate and deserving of any bouquets she receives on Grandparents Day. Rita gingerly stepped into her new role after the loss of her sister and brother-in-law, picking up some of their grandparenting responsibilities along the way. Rita loves it. Her grandnieces take turns spending the night with their well-loved aunt and regularly invite her to special school and sporting events. The girls are busy with swim meets and tennis lessons, parties and play dates, but my friend is a major player in their life, just as any grandparent would be. As she grows older, Rita values their presence more and more.

"I don't see them nearly as much as I'd like to," she admits, but every moment that she does is precious to her. People like Rita, surrogate grandparents who fill a need or mend a loss, are essential elements in the network of grandparents who surround and uphold today's families.

Our old friends Rose and Lou have four children and seven grandchildren to keep them out of trouble. They're never short of words when the subject is politics or religion. But they become positively tongue-tied when they try to articulate the tender feelings their grandchildren evoke.

"There's nothing terribly profound about our relationship with the kids," Rose says modestly. "Just getting everyone together and seeing them interacting, being a family, gives me a warm feeling." Prodded, Rose will tell you about young Jack, almost two. "He adores me," she murmurs. "He thinks I'm the best thing that ever happened to him."

Lou says the whole thing hits him when the family gathers for their annual Octoberfest of birthdays. There are so many that month that they celebrate with a big dinner at the grandparents' house. "I look down at the table, at these seventeen people all gathered around me," he says, lifting his hands in surrender, "and I ask myself, *What have I done?*"

I sometimes wonder the same thing. It's a real miracle, this gift of grandchildren, part of an unbroken circle that keeps on growing, keeps on giving, even when I think my worn, cracked plate is full.

A local artist, a potter whose self-styled "earthbound urns" are a source of pleasure and amusement to those who collect her whimsical work, finds her place in time and space by tracing her own circle of life back to her grandmother. Rosemary's father was a lawyer, her mother an artist, so she spent much of her time at her grandparents' home while her parents worked. A younger Rosemary slept in her grandparents' bed, tended their garden, and romped with them through carefree days in the picturesque foothills of the Appalachians, where her extended family lived and flourished.

"Art was just everywhere," Rosemary recalled, and her grandmother Agnes was a powerful influence on the family's artistic tradition. "She was," said her granddaughter, "the center of the wheel."

Agnes painted and sculpted, played the piano, plucked the fiddle. As a teacher of art and later a librarian in local schools, she gave back what she'd been given. Her creativity was like a strong, guiding arm that stretched out and gently pointed the way so others could follow. Her sense of humor was handed on as well, Rosemary said. It was a bright torch that lit the family's road to the ridiculous.

"One Thanksgiving we were turkeys from outer space," Rosemary remembered. "Then there was the time we dressed up as Indians and had a pow-wow, camping out in a turnip patch and eating squash casserole cooked over a fire." Christmas holidays were excuses for further merriment. A homemade movie of *Cinderella*, featuring her uncles in drag as the wicked stepsisters and her grandfather in boxer shorts as the fairy godmother, was one of their best efforts. "The women were the chorus, singing on the sidelines, so we could just laugh and watch them carry on."

Agnes' affinity for the lighter side of life imbues her granddaughter's art today. Fanciful faces with oversized noses, stuck-out tongues, and rolling eyeballs peer from Rosemary's softly glazed pots and jugs. Grinning mouths and sardonic expressions capture a side of clay few artists have explored. Her body of work has been described as amusing, ironic, witty, playful. It's also been appraised as technically sound and creatively advanced. It's her grandmother's legacy that has lent passion and direction to Rosemary's art and she is grateful.

In memory of her grandmother, Rosemary and five other members of her family recently undertook a mixed media exhibit entitled *Agnes' Women*. The show, held at a downtown gallery, represented three generations of this gifted family's artistic endeavors. There were welded sculptures by Rosemary's mother and painting and photography studies by her cousin and aunts. Rosemary's pottery was displayed, along with a number of larger wall hangings that demonstrated the range of her talent. The opening reception, at which inappropriate attire was roundly encouraged, was a festive tribute to Agnes's light and fulsome spirit.

Foolish hats and outlandish costumes prevailed. False eyelashes and Hawaiian shirts mingled with goofy footwear. One family member, demurely dressed in a neon tutu that was too tight in all the wrong places, sported an odd dusting of little white feathers glued randomly to her bare shoulders. She was obviously the one who had painted the outrageous portraits of dancing chickens: *Hen in Tights, Chickens on Stage, Arabesque.* Rosemary's own works of clay seemed to wink slyly—perhaps even conspiratorially—at the crush of friends and patrons who had gathered to wish Agnes's women well.

No doubt Agnes would have approved of all this silliness. She would have taken pride in her granddaughter's art and humor, in the spiritual underpinnings of her descendants' work. Had she been there, Agnes would probably have put on a wacky costume and partied with the rest of us. From all reports, this free-spirited grandmother had a sublime sense of fun.

I'm not one of Agnes' women, but I can taste the kind of joy and freedom her creative family continues to enjoy. With the help of my grandchildren, I can, like Agnes, cultivate life's lighter side and make a place for it in my heart. If I listen for the music and practice my steps, I'll be ready when the band starts to play.

*Grandchildren invite us to laugh and celebrate, to sing and to dance. The presence of a grandchild means joy is at hand, wonder is within reach. The gift of grandparenting unfolds as I open my heart to its possibilities.*

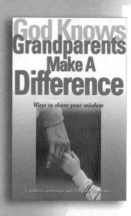

**Thea Jarvis** has written for numerous periodicals including *The Atlanta Constitution*, *America Magazine*, *Catholic Digest*, and Catholic News Service. For nineteen years she wrote for the *Georgia Bulletin*, Atlanta's Catholic weekly newspaper. Her family life column was featured in seventeen diocesan newspapers. This is her first book.